MOHAMED MAKIYA

ALSO BY KAREN DABROWSKA

Iraq: The Ancient Sites and Iraqi Kurdistan

Melancholy Memories, Foreign Dreams

The Libyan Revolution: Diary of Qadhafi's Newsgirl in London

Into the Abyss: Human Rights Violations in Bahrain and the Suppression of the Popular Movement for Change

Addis Ababa: A Pocket Guide to Ethiopia's Capital City

MOHAMED MAKIYA

A Modern Architect Renewing Islamic Tradition

Karen Dabrowska

SAQI

SAQI BOOKS
26 Westbourne Grove
London W2 5RH
www.saqibooks.com

Published 2021 by Saqi Books

Copyright © Karen Dabrowska 2021

Karen Dabrowska has asserted her right under the Copyright, Designs
and Patents Act, 1988, to be identified as the author of this work.

Map on p. 11 'The Baghdad of Mohamed Makiya's early life'
produced by Zaid Isam, 2020.

This book is sold subject to the condition that it shall not, by way of trade
or otherwise, be lent, resold, hired out, or otherwise circulated without the
publisher's prior consent in any form of binding or cover other than that in
which it is published and without a similar condition including this condition
being imposed on the subsequent purchaser.

ISBN 978 0 86356 416 1
eISBN 978 0 86356 481 9

A full CIP record for this book is available from the British Library.

Printed and bound by CPI Group (UK) Ltd, Croydon CR0 4YY

This book was made possible by a grant from the
Makiya-Kufa Charity for the arts in the Middle East.

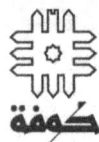

This book is dedicated to Sheikh Dr Ibrahim El Tayeb El Rayah and his family.

If architecture is to be an art exercising a positive influence towards the good, then an attempt must be made to discuss its relevance to ethical values of society, traditional values of time and the cultural values of space: these three considerations make up the fundamental basis of its comprehensive scholarly understanding needed in face of present chaotic mannerisms.

Mohamed Saleh Makiya, 'Architecture and the Mediterranean Climate: Studies on the Effect of Climatic Conditions on Architectural Development in the Mediterranean Region with Special Reference to the Prospects of Its Practice in the "Near East"' (Abstract, PhD dissertation, King's College, Cambridge, 1945)

CONTENTS

Acknowledgments xiii
Timeline xv

Preface 1
1. Beginnings: Sababigh al-Aal, Baghdad 7
2. The Liverpool Years 21
3. The Cambridge Years 32
4. Return to Iraq 40
5. Mohamed and Margaret in Baghdad 49
6. The Iraqi Artists' Society 60
7. The Khulafa Mosque 74
8. The School of Architecture 80
9. Leaving Baghdad 96
10. Makiya Associates and Architecture in Exile 107
11. The Baghdad State Mosque 134
12. The Kufa Gallery and the Sultan Qaboos Mosque 148
13. Conflict and Reconciliation 166
14. Makiya's Legacy 177

Postscript 191
Appendices 201
　I. Abstract of Makiya's PhD Thesis 203
　II. Lecture by Mohamed Makiya: 'Arab Architecture
　　　Past and Present' 207
　III. Address to The Centenary of the Iraqi Architect
　　　Mohamed Makiya held in conjunction with the
　　　Baghdad Capital of Culture Festivities in 2014 213

Notes 215
Bibliography 221
Index 223

Acknowledgments

This publication was made possible due to a generous grant from the Makiya Kufa Foundation.

First and foremost I would like to thank Kanan Makiya for giving me the opportunity to write a biography of his father Mohamed Makiya.

Special thanks to Robert Cohen for editing the manuscript, Dr Abdul Rahim Hassan for his encouragement, support and valuable comments on the text. Thanks also to Lindsay Fulcher, Jonathan Derrick and Tim Frost.

For interviews, information, anecdotes and valuable insights into Dr Makiya's character I would like to thank Hind Makiya, Amal Makiya, Ghassan Makiya, Naseem Makiya, Ali Mousawi, Ahmed Naji al-Said, Akram Ogaily, Dr Iain Jackson, Dia Kashi, Subhi al-Azzawi, Attared Sarraf, Ghada al-Silq, Mustafa al-Kazimy, Khaled Sultani, Khaled Kashtiny, Professor Stephen Kite, Zina Allawi, Harvey Morris, Godfrey Heaps, Garry Martin, Diddi Malek, Rose Issa, Hussein Sikafi, Yasmine Allawi, Fran Hazelton, Mahdi Ali, Rashid al-Khayoun, Maysoon Wahbi and the late Lamia Gailani.

Unless otherwise stated, quotations are from interviews conducted by the author.

TIMELINE

	Makiya	Iraq
1534–1918		Iraq part of Ottoman Empire
1914	Makiya born in Baghdad	
1918		British defeat at Kut
1920		Britain creates state of Iraq
1921	Makiya's father dies – Makiya lives with uncle	
1932		Iraq becomes independent state
1935	Arrives in UK for studies	
1939–45		Britain reoccupies Iraq
1941	Studies for degree in architecture at Liverpool University – meets future wife	
1942	Gets a diploma in Civil Engineering from Liverpool University, UK	
1946	Gets doctorate from Cambridge Returns to Baghdad – establishes Makiya Associates	
1947–53	Architect for Directorate of Municipalities	
1949	Son Kanan born	
1951	Writes *The Arab Village* Appointed UN expert for seminar on social welfare in Arab countries	

1952	Daughter Hind born	
1955–59	President, Iraqi Arts Society	
1956	Fulbright Scholar	
1957	Escorts Iraqi regent through first modern art exhibition	
1958		Iraqi monarchy overthrown
1959	Builds own house in Baghdad Sets up Dept of Architecture, Baghdad University	
1960–65	Designs Khulafa Mosque, Baghdad	
1961	Drives from Baghdad to Moscow	
1963		Abd al-Karim Qasim ousted in Baathist coup
1965	Plan for Baghdad University	
1966	Theology College Baghdad design	
1967	Plan for Kufa University. Opens office in Bahrain. President, Iraqi Architectural Association	
1968	Kufa university project shut. Wins competition for Bahrain Chamber of Commerce	Baathist coup
1969	Writes 'Architecture of Baghdad'	
1970	Designs mosques in Pakistan	
1971	Relocates to Bahrain after being exiled from Baathist Iraq Opens Muscat Office	
1972		Iraq nationalises Petroleum Company
1973	In Bahrain designs mosque, Sheikh Mubarak Building, Centre for Handicapped	

1974	Opens office in UK. Designs Hilton in UAE	
1975	Opens office in Doha Designs Kuwait State Mosque	
1976	Plans for Kuwait State Mosque	
1980–88		Iran-Iraq war
1980	Agrees to Saddam Hussein's invitation to redesign Baghdad. Son Kanan resigns from Makiya Associates	
1981	Designs complex of Rashid University in Iraq. Member of Steering Committee for Aga Khan Architectural Awards	
1983	Designs Baghdad State Mosque, El Andalous Housing Complex, Baghdad Arab League Headquarters	
1984	Public lecture at Royal Institute of British Architects. Designs parade ground in Tikrit	
1986	Interior design, police officers' club. Kufa Gallery opens in London	
1987	Completes Design of Regional Arab Organisations in Kuwait	
1988	Breaks links with Saddam Hussein	
1989	Kanan Makiya publishes *Republic of Fear* under a pseudonym	
1990		Iraq invades Kuwait
1991	Kanan Makiya publishes *The Monuments* under a pseudonym	First Gulf War
1997	Design consultant on Sultan Qaboos Mosque	

2003		Second Gulf War
2004		US hands sovereignty to interim government
2005		Voters approve constitution
2006	Kufa Gallery closed	Average of 100 civilians killed every day
2008		
2010		Parliamentary elections
2011	Archive donated to MIT	US completes troop pull-out
2012	Wife Margaret dies	
2013	Honoured during Baghdad Capital of Culture celebrations	
2014	Receives 100th birthday card from Queen. Khalid Al-Sultani publishes *Mohamed Makiya: A Century of Architecture and Life*	ISIS seizes Mosul. Haider Al Abad forms broad-based government. ISIS destroys Nimurd and Hatra
2015	Dies in London	

Preface

'Makiya was Baghdad and Baghdad was Makiya.' These seven words from Akram Ogaily, a former student and later a colleague of Dr Mohamed Makiya, sum up the life of one of the Middle East's most famous modern architects, whose career spanned seven decades and included projects in more than ten countries. Makiya's work showed that traditional Islamic styles can be incorporated into modern architecture, as seen in his greatest work, the restoration of a ninth-century minaret and the design of a mosque around it. 'Simplicity with dignity' was his motto and his guiding principle.

Makiya died in London on 19 July 2015, aged 101. When he was 100 years old he stayed awake at night crying for his beloved city, which has been plagued by sectarian violence following the 2003 war. He composed a moving tribute to his city which was was heard in Baghdad by participants at a one-day conference: 'The Centenary of the Iraqi architect Mohamed Makiya', held in conjunction with the Baghdad Capital of Culture festivities in 2014. At the age of 100 he was not able to travel to the conference but he was there is spirit: on the podium from which conference participants spoke was a giant black-and-white image of Mohamed Makiya, who gazed approvingly at the speakers as they listened attentively to his message:

> Cities have souls, and these are tangible souls that can be sniffed and sensed, in every place. Baghdad is dear and priceless. When we were forced to leave it, many years ago, we knew that some of our soul stayed there on the banks of the Tigris, in the city's alleyways, coffee-shops, balconies and squares. We knew that we had part of Baghdad with us. It grew with us like our children. We grew old and to a ripe old age. This centenary is on its way out, but that thing, that part of Baghdad, will not grow old. It is not going to get to a ripe old age. It is united

with our dreams, our dialect, our way of thinking. It climbs the walls of our houses. It metamorphoses into a kind Iraqi sun that is warm in the severe cold winter days and provides a nice cold breeze from the Tigris during summer days.

Mohamed Makiya was born as the Ottoman Empire, of which Iraq was a part, was disintegrating; Iraq became a British colony, with a monarch installed by Britain. During this period Makiya studied in the UK before returning home to set up Makiya Associates. The firm grew from strength to strength. In 1971, however, his integrity was wrongly called into question by conspiracy theorists within the Baathist regime. Though he was forced into exile, his architectural practice thrived in the Gulf. In 1981 all was forgiven and he was welcomed back to Baghdad to modernise the capital. Eventually the lucrative contracts from Iraq and the Gulf dried up, whereupon Makiya set up the Kufa Gallery, an oasis of Middle Eastern culture in London. When the gallery closed in 2006 he retired to his flat in central London, where he continued to make plans for a prosperous Iraq – a future that he never saw.

Mohamed Makiya shines in three constellations of gifted men. First and foremost he was an architect, a master of incorporating traditional styles into modern architecture and a form-giver to Middle Eastern architecture. His most important work was an extension to the Khulafa Mosque in Baghdad, completed in 1963, in which the old and new mosques were integrated in a harmonious design featuring a minaret from the ninth century. There was a continuation of tradition in all his work, even though it was executed with modern materials. His architecture was a link between the past and the present, metamorphising dead Abbasid forms into living modern architecture. For him Islamic architecture was the architecture of freedom and of the future. In a public lecture to the Royal Institute of British Architects in 1984 he stated that unity in diversity and simplicity with dignity are the basic characteristics of Arab architecture and Islamic urbanism when they are at their very best. The continuity of tradition as a 'living dimension' was the justification for his work.

Second, he was a great teacher who inspired hundreds of students of architecture. The first Iraqi to get a PhD in architecture, he was eager to pass on his knowledge. He was a hard taskmaster, demanding nothing but the best from those he taught, but they loved him as a father and spoke affectionately of him as if they were his children. In 1959 he set up the first Department of Architecture in Baghdad University, producing generations of Iraqi architects who were very much in tune with Iraqi architectural heritage and also with modern architecture. His students from the period of his professorship in Baghdad represent almost as impressive a legacy as his buildings. In his memory the Mohamed Makiya Prize for Architecture is awarded every year to the individual or organisation that has made the greatest contribution to the advancement of Iraqi architecture.

And, third, he was a collector and promoter of Iraqi art, which he displayed with pride and enthusiasm in London's Kufa Gallery, which he set up in 1986 to build a bridge between the East and the West.

He incorporated calligraphy into his buildings; he opened a gallery in his office in Baghdad; and as the first president of the Iraqi Artists' Society he ensured the arts were patronised both by the monarchy and by Abd al-Karim Qasim's government which overthrew the monarchy in 1958. He was always looking at orientalist paintings and was intrigued by how building form was created in a typical Middle Eastern environment.

Apart from his wife there were three great loves in his life: Baghdad, humanity and the Shi'i culture and traditions. He was overjoyed when he had the opportunity to present a design for one of the grandest architectural competitions ever sponsored in a country of the Third World. The brief was for a state mosque. It was commissioned by Saddam Hussein and Makiya refuted criticism of working for Saddam with the comment: 'This is for history. It's not for the people there now [the Baathists]. It's got nothing to do with them –

they'll be gone. This is for the future,' he would tell colleagues and friends.

He was a socialiser, the life of the party, and he took an interest in people; everyone from his drivers to the Aga Khan loved him. In the words of Rudyard Kipling he could talk with crowds and keep his virtue, and he would walk with kings and not lose his common touch. He was always compassionate. He had the intelligence of the heart and the intelligence of the eye. Humility and vitality beyond all imagination characterised Makiya's personality, and these qualities were impressed upon those who came into contact with him.

Ahmed Naji al-Said, author of *Under the Palm Trees: Modern Iraqi Art with Mohamed Makiya and Jewad Selim*, told me:

> When you meet Makiya you are meeting somebody who is truly Baghdadi – the words he uses, his tone, the facial expression, the warmth he exudes. Whenever he met someone he would always make that person feel important and feel that he is welcome. For Makiya there was always something better that the present generation could do for the future. 'You should not just be happy and satisfied with the status quo,' he would say. 'You should always find something that will inspire the next generation.' He was a man from a medieval city living in modern times. He lived in this turning point of time when cultures met, when the British were in Iraq and he was an Iraqi in Britain. That is what helped to shape his character and his thinking.

This biography tells the story of Dr Mohamed Saleh Makiya's life. He was a visionary and a dreamer and some of his dreams came true: the restoration of the Khulafa mosque and minaret, the setting up of the Department of Architecture at Baghdad University, the establishment of the Kufa Gallery. His philosophy and his humanity crossed all borders, cultures and continents. Above all he was a humanitarian who cared about the welfare of his fellow human beings. His life story is intrinsically connected to the story of Baghdad and Iraq.

There are few champions of Baghdad who love the city like their dearest friend and care for it like a wayward child. When Makiya passed on it was a dark day for the place that its founder, the Abbasid caliph Abu Jafar al-Mansur, named 'the City of Peace'. Tragically today it is a city of war. Only time will tell if it will become the tranquil city that Makiya saw in his dreams. He never lost hope, and this hope inspired thousands of Iraqis. After his death he became the hero they were searching for. But who was Mohamed Makiya?

CHAPTER I

Beginnings: Sabbabigh al-Aal, Baghdad

'I never had to read about a medieval city, because I lived in one ... I'm very much influenced by it. I'm deeply Baghdadi, and I've been thinking of Baghdad all my life.'

Baghdad was once a circular, walled city with four gates – Kufa, Basra, Khurasan and Syria – named because they pointed in the directions of these destinations. Today, only the Wastani Gate exists, and it has been restored twice in modern times.

According to John Warren and Ihsan Fethi, authors of *Traditional Houses in Baghdad*: 'Flood, decay and city-planners together destroyed almost all parts of the city [that] were built before 1890. With the exception of a scattering of old mosques and of two much restored thirteenth-century structures (the Abbasid Palace and the Mustansiriya School), the city of Baghdad dates from the end of the First World War (1918).' This was the Baghdad, a city of change and transition, into which Mohamed Makiya was born in 1914.

Mohamed Makiya's mother used to say that her son was born the year the British entered Baghdad. But the British actually entered it twice, the first time in 1914 and the second in 1917; it is generally assumed that Mohamed was born on 5 November 1914.[1]

Mohamed loved Baghdad, the so-called 'City of Peace', whose story is in fact largely a tale of continuous war – and where there was not war, there was pestilence, famine and civil disturbance. Nestling in the Tigris-Euphrates valley, the Baghdad area attracted settlements from pre-Islamic times. But by the eighth century it had become the capital of the Muslim world. Between 1258, after having been destroyed by Mongol invaders, the Persians and Turks vied for control of the city, until in 1638 it became a bulwark of the Ottoman Empire.

Having retaken the city from the Persians, the Turks eagerly sought the loyalty of the citizens. Although the Persians invaded Iraq again in 1818, a cholera epidemic halted their progress. British Lieutenant Henry Lynch journeyed up and down the Tigris River from 1837 to 1842 and established the Euphrates and Tigris Steam Navigation Company. The late nineteenth century brought new technology and new ideas of progress: trains and steamships were introduced, along with the telegraph, and oil exploration began. Trade and commerce flourished, and by 1900 Baghdad was three times the size it had been in 1830.

✦

As Turkish influence declined, European influence increased. During the First World War, Baghdad became a Turkish base of operations against the British. The Turks finally left the city in 1917, but not before the military commandant destroyed as many official records as he could. The Talisman Gate was blown up as a parting gesture.

The British were not impressed by what they saw: miserable, dilapidated houses of mud-brown brick, along with narrow, filthy streets. The smell was putrid and the starving dogs looked menacing. The British military police reportedly shot 4,917 diseased animals.[2] The army did not leave immediately, even though the threatened Turkish return never took place. A new city administration took over the running of Baghdad; electricity and sanitation were introduced; and improvements were made to the streets and the water supply. (In 1925, al-Rashid Street would be the first thoroughfare in Baghdad to be paved for vehicles.) There was an ambitious programme of bridge-building, road repairs and irrigation, documented in great detail in the ten-volume Iraq Administration Reports of 1914–32. The British also made themselves comfortable in their clubs, where they played polo, tennis, cricket, football and golf.

At the very time Mohamed was growing up, the British were constructing the entity that would thereafter be known as Iraq. In 1920–21, Basra, Baghdad and Mosul were lumped together, with the Sunni amir Faisal I bin Hussein bin Ali al-Hashemi installed as king. Though he was committed to pan-Arabism and sought to create unity between Sunni and Shi'i within his administration, Faisal's ambitions were frustrated by the British, who controlled Iraq under a League of Nations mandate until the end of 1932. The tensions thus exacerbated were not resolved by independence, and Faisal I died only a year into the post-mandate era. His son, Ghazi, was killed in an accident after six unsettled years in power, to be nominally replaced by his own four-year-old son, Faisal II, with the reins actually held by Abd al-Ilah, a pro-British regent.

❧

Sabbabigh al-Aal, the district of of Old Baghdad where Mohamed Makiya was born, was a largely Shi'i community, but shared by Christians and Jews. They dwelt together in the shadow of a crumbling but still impressive minaret – all that remained of the brick-built, thirteenth-century mosque of al-Ghazl. 'We lived in a prominent neighbourhood called Suq al-Ghazl,' Makiya told the author Guy Mannes-Abbott, 'very central, and close to something called the Weaver's Mosque that went back to the Abbasid period and Baghdad's founding. Our family was a prominent weaving family. My father would get materials from the Silk Route and from China. He was one of the main dealers, and my cousin had one of the best shops in Baghdad for textiles. Later [my father] started bringing [materials] from Italy, but before that we brought everything from Aleppo, Syria, because the industry there was very good. Modernity first came to Iraq from Damascus, Syria, and the Mediterranean.'[3]

Makiya's life was a melting pot of influences: trade and travel as well as religion and family. His father, Hadji Saleh Aziz Makiya, had a lot of customers from the villages outside Baghdad. They would come once or twice a year to buy clothing from him, because they trusted him. When there was famine or very little rain he would allow them to pay when conditions improved, rather than make them sell property to pay their bills. Therefore they could maintain their farms and their livelihoods.

Saleh Makiya's business dealings involved journeys on the Silk Route from Samarkand. Using these trade routes brought his father into contact with foreign companies that travelled along the Tigris and Euphrates – so when Mohamed was selected for study abroad, even though he had never travelled any distance himself, the notion of imported knowledge was not entirely foreign to him.

Mohamed spoke extensively to Iraqi author, journalist and biographer Rashid al-Khayoun about his childhood and early life, and al-Khayoun recorded these conversations and turned them into a book (*Reflections on the Years: Biography of an Architect and the Diary of a Baghdadi Neighbourhood*).* Mohamed told al-Khayoun that the family traced its origins to Arabia. He remarked that his mother's family came from southern Iraq and that they were visited by one Safia, an aunt from the south who was a well-known vernacular poet able to engage in poetic debates, and skilful enough to intimidate the famous poet Khabout al-Kharki. She told many interesting stories, which left the young Mohamed enthralled.

According to Mohamed's niece Amal, Safia later moved to Baghdad. 'She was the only aunt Mohamed had from his father's side,' Amal told me. 'She had a remarkable ability to create. She would sit with you and then she would recite an original poem. We don't have a picture of her. There were no photos in those days.' Mohamed was sad that he did not record any of Safia's memories. At that time he was not interested in biographical details. 'Living abroad stripped me of those memories,' he told al-Khayoun.

There are a number of different stories about the origin of the family name Makiya. Women were so important in the textile trade

---

* Translation from the Arabic text.

Beginnings: Sababigh al-Aal, Baghdad   11

The Baghdad of Mohamed Makiya's early life

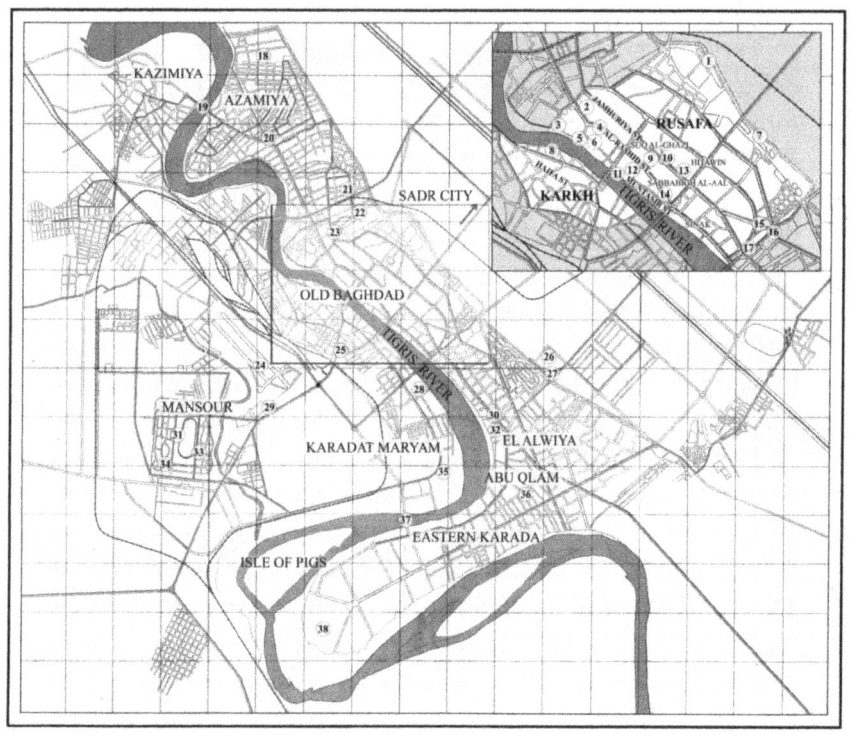

1 The Wastani Gate; 2 National library; 3 Al-Amana hall; 4 Umm Kulthum and Al-Zahawi cafés; 5 The Abbasid Palace and 6 Al-Markazia secondary schools; 7 The Talisman Gate; 8 The women's hospital; 9 Shurja souks; 10 Suq al-Ghazl minaret; 11 Mustansiriya School; 12 Bezzarzeen souk; 13 Al-Hashimea primary school; 14 Lynch Company; 15 The Modern Art Museum 16 The Freedom Mural by Faiq Hassan; 17 Nasb al-Hurriyya (Freedom Monument); 18 Baghdad College; 19 Jisr al-Aima; 20 The Olympic Club; 21 The British Council School; 22 The College of Theology; 23 School of Architecture, Baghdad University; 24 Baghdad State Mosque; 25 Iraqi Museum; 26 Olympic-sized stadium; 27 Saddam Hussein Gymnasium; 28 Parliament House; 29 Building of Iraqi Artists' Society; 30 Unknown Soldier Monument; 31 Al-Mansour Club; 32 El Alwiya club; 33 The house of Princess Badeea; 34 American High School; 35 The royal palace; 36 Al-Sharqia secondary schools; 37 Suspension bridge; 38 Campus of Baghdad University.

at the beginning of the twentieth century that the name of the husband was often dropped, leaving the wife's name. This may have been the case in Mohamed's family.

The name could have Arabian origins from Mecca. Another story, or legend, tells of a woman called Makiya who was alive 150 years before Mohamed was born. She lived in Arabia and is said to have been surprised in her tent by a bunch of thieves, whom she battled. She grabbed one of the thieves, dragged him to the head of the tribe, and denounced him – and the members of the tribe were so impressed by her courage and strength that they named the family after her. In the account that Mohamed gave to al-Khayoun, his own family took its name from a female relation by marriage who distinguished herself in the spinning and weaving trade. This, by his calculations, would have been towards the end of the seventeenth century.

Mohamed was the son of Hadji Saleh Aziz Makiya and his third wife, Bahiya, who also gave birth to his brother, Abdul Aziz. Saleh Makiya's first wife had four children, three boys and one girl, and his second wife was childless. He married Bahiya when he was in his fifties and she was in her early twenties. Mohamed never really knew his father, who died when he was two years old. His mother lavished all her affection on him and his brother, and this love sustained him during his childhood and teenage years. His mother also nurtured his love and respect for the Muslim faith. She could recite the Qur'an by heart and taught it to the children in the neighbourhood. But she also respected other religions, and encouraged Mohamed to run errands for their Jewish neighbours on Saturday (the Jewish Sabbath).

When Mohamed was four years old he suffered from a persistent undiagnosed high fever, and Bahiya vowed that when her son recovered he would commemorate *Ashura* (a day of remembrance on the 10th of Muharram), when Shi'i Muslims atone for the murder of Hussein.

'My father had a reputation as a pious and trustworthy businessman of the Baghdad textile souk, a neighbourhood figure whose house would always be open to the public during the month of

Ramadan,' Mohamed recalled when discussing his memories with Maureen Kubba, who began writing his biography.[4] 'Although [my father] died when I was only two years of age, he left me a legacy of interrelation, tolerance and resourcefulness.'

Mohamed himself was steeped in his family's Shi'ism from birth, not in its strict religiosity but in its festive spirit. For him religion was not so much a question of faith as one of culture – a link with his ancestors. Though proud of being Shi'i he was a 'light Muslim', who did not pray five times a day, enjoyed a drink, respected other faiths, and would in time come to celebrate Christmas with his family. Mohamed wanted to bring the Shi'i imams into the twenty-first century and commented that their turbans had closed their thinking. 'They can cover their head but not their brain,' he once said with a smile.

❦

The family traded through the Lynch Company, whose building in Mustansir Street stood next to the one that housed ther own office. The Makiyas had a warehouse for wool and made extensive contacts with wool weavers and merchants in Syria. A member of the family named Khazal married a Syrian woman and facilitated trade with Aleppo. They were also involved in the silk trade and imported silk and other goods from China. The fabrics would come to the port of Basra, where the legendary Silk Road ended.

Other family members imported cloth from Italy. Mohamed's father, who was known as *haji* (someone who had made the pilgrimage to Mecca), also had a guesthouse, which was used as a meeting place for social and political gatherings. It was especially busy during Ramadan and Muharram.* When Saleh Makiya died, his brother, Mahdi, tried to exploit the business for his own advantage and opened a shop in another area, but the business failed.

---

* An annual celebration in the month of Muharram commemorating the death of Hussein, grandson of Muhammad, and his retinue.

Mohamed Makiya (left) with Uncle Aboud and Aboud's children. (Pic Amal Makiya)

When Mohamed's father died, the family went to live with Saleh's uncle Aboud – his mother's brother, a grocer – who had a house in the same neighbourhood. Aboud was a burly man with a knife in his belt and a menacing air about him. One day when Mohamed, aged twelve, was at secondary school, Aboud appeared, grabbed him by the arm, and said, 'Enough of this – I need you in the shop.' He frog-marched his nephew out of the classroom and put him to work. But the next day the headmaster of Mohamed's school, a thin, frail Jewish man named Salim Hakim who wore a *sadara* (Ottoman hat), came to the shop, berated Aboud in front of his customers and fellow shopkeepers for not appreciating the value of education, called him an ignoramus, and dragged Mohamed back to school. In the end, Mohamed would stay in school until he completed his baccalaureate at the age of eighteen. When his beloved headmaster died, Mohamed paid homage to him at the Kufa Gallery in London, the institution that he set up in the 1980s.

Life with the extended family was not without tension and in 1928 Mohamed, along with his mother and brother, moved into their own house.

❧

Growing up in Baghdad, Mohamed always lived close to the Tigris. The river is eloquently described by Freya Stark in *Baghdad Sketches*:

> The width of the Tigris in Baghdad is about 400 yards, a noble stream. It is the only sweet and fresh thoroughfare of the town: not clear water, but lion-coloured, like Tiber or Arno. Its broad flowing surface is dyed by the same earth of which the houses and minarets on its banks are built, so that all is one tawny harmony. Its low winter mists in early morning, or yellow slabs of sunset shallows when the water buffaloes come down to drink after the day; its many craft, evolved through centuries so that one looks upon an epitome of the history of ships from the earliest days of mankind; the barefoot traffic of its banks, where the women come with jars upon their shoulders and boatmen tow their vessels against the current: all this was a perpetual joy.

Describing the Baghdad of his childhood, Mohamed observed: 'It was like the Middle Ages. I never had to read about a medieval city, because I lived in one. There was no electricity, no water, no sanitation. I'm very much influenced by it. I'm deeply Baghdadi, and I've been thinking of Baghdad all my life.'[5]

When he was growing up Mohamed did not pay much attention to the family home, but it later exerted a major influence on his architectural designs. 'It was a masterful study of space. How could an area of less than 200 metres house five families? There was

The Katah Bridge over the River Tigris circa early 1930s
Matson (G. Eric and Edith) Photograph Collection

Lorna Selim, Makiya's childhood house in Baghdad, 1990 (Pic: Ahmed Naji)

Beginnings: Sababigh al-Aal, Baghdad

a central court and a *diwan* (salon) and a basement. There was a large entrance and within it a place to sit so that somebody could read the Qur'an if they wanted to. Above, there were five rooms, but the roof was a sleeping space. I learned then that the sky is a roof itself. The whole idea of the house was very important to me.'[6]

Mohamed's primary school was al-Hashimea, a private school that was part of the Jaffariyya schools: a network of modern schools for the Shi'i formed during the last days of the Ottoman Empire. 'It was different from the homogeneous bureaucratic government schools,' Mohamed recalled. 'It was a school of and for the district.'[7] His brother, Abdul Aziz, was four years older than Mohamed, and they were not in the same classes throughout their primary and secondary education.

Mohamed was a compassionate child. His pet lamb would follow him on his trips to market, and he pampered it with special food; the family could not bring themselves to tell Mohamed when it had been slaughtered. A cat once came to Mohamed's aid when he was asleep and bit off the head of a snake which was coming toward him.

After primary school, in 1930, Mohamed went to two secondary schools: for the first three years to al-Sharqia and for the last two years to al-Markazia, a progressive institution. He was fortunate to have enlightened teachers, including Mustafa Jawad, an Arabic linguist and historian, and Jawad Ali, a historian and author of *The Abridged History of the Arabs before Islam*. Sadiq al-Malaikah taught drama and set up a theatre where Shakespeare's plays were performed. The school also devoted a lot of time to art lessons and organised exhibitions. The older students taught the younger students drawing: Mohamed was taught by Midhat Ali Madloum, later to become a prominent architect.

Mohamed was an exceptional student: brilliant at mathematics, and earning one of the highest marks in the country in the baccalaureate exams required for admission to college. He was very lucky that, just as he was about to leave school, the Minister of Education instituted a programme to send fifty of the brightest students to various European countries on all-expenses-paid government scholarships.

Mohamed applied for a scholarship in petroleum engineering. His brother, Abdul Aziz, encouraged him to do so, so that he could work in an industry run by the the oil companies themselves, outside government control. But his application was rejected, because the companies, not the ministry, were responsible for oil scholarships.

Sati al-Hursi, the Director General of Education, then recommended Mohamed's studying mathematics in Germany, but Mohamed refused because he didn't know the language – and he did not want to do advanced study in mathematics, even though mathematics had been his major in secondary school. Instead he applied to the medical college in Baghdad where his brother, Abdul Aziz, was studying.

But events soon led to his being chosen for a scholarship after all. Sadiq al-Bassam, the Minister of Education, sent for Mohamed. The minster asked him why he refused to go to Germany, and Mohamed explained why. Al-Bassam then asked al-Husri to give him the oil scholarship, but was told that al-Husri had no power to do this. He then told al-Husri to give Mohamed a scholarship to study architecture in Britain.

※

In November 1935 Mohamed left Iraq to study in Britain. His mother prepared food for him to take on the journey. The family was sad, but he had no regrets: he was ambitious and eager to pursue his studies abroad.

The first stop on the journey to London was Damascus, where Mohamed's cousin Kadhim was working as a trader. Mohamed travelled by Nairn Eastern Transport Company vehicle across the Syrian desert, where the only road was the tracks made by vehicles that had previously undertaken the journey. The Nairn Brothers, Gerald and Norman, of New Zealand origin and possibly Scottish ancestry, had served in the British army during the First World War. Before the war they had run a motorcycle dealership in New Zealand, and they were experienced and knowledgeable mechanics. They saw a business opportunity to sell cars in the Middle East and a Beirut family backed them in this endeavour, which led them to explore the feasibility of crossing the Syrian desert by car. Their solution became very popular and was used by famous writers and other celebrated people, including Gertrude Bell,[*] Freya Stark,[†] and Agatha Christie. Heavily loaded small cars and lorries frequently made the journey.

The car sped along the sand, stopping at a guesthouse en route that had the air of an English country club, and where a first-rate Western-style meal was provided. British people returning from leave when serving in the colonies felt at home in this little slice of England. Local sheikhs offered protection from bandits and robbers and assured travellers of a safe passage.

For Mohamed, the car journey to Beirut was an eye-opener. It was the first time he had seen mountains or the sea, and the scenery proved such a revelation that he determined never to let the earth's beauties and wonders pass him by.

He boarded a French ship, the *Champignon Marseilles*, which sailed via Port Said in Egypt, stopping in Malta before arriving in Marseilles. Mohamed compared the restaurant on the ship to that in a first-class hotel.

From Marseilles, Mohamed and the countrymen he met en route travelled to Paris, arriving at dawn to find boys and girls embracing each other in the streets and the cafés still open. Though they adapted quickly to their surroundings, they soon realised that in Europe they were perceived as primitive. Mohamed met two Iraqi

---

[*] Gertrude Bell was an extraordinary Oriental Secretary with the British Administration in Iraq. She was the first woman to achieve a First Class Honours in Modern History at Oxford.
[†] Freya Stark, a famous British explorer and travel writer, lived in Baghdad during the 1920s.

artists, Faiq Hassan and Jewad Salim, at the Tunisian coffee shop in the Latin Quarter, and started to gain an appreciation of the arts.

Salim, who became Mohamed's lifelong friend, was living at the Sorbonne and studying with Hassan. Mohamed remembered meeting them frequently at a small restaurant near the Sorbonne. One evening Salim brought his classical guitar and started playing. Mohamed held out his hat and pretended they were buskers.

After Marseilles, some of the students left for Germany, while Mohamed proceeded to Calais and took the ferry to Dover. The journey ended at London's Victoria Station, where Mohamed's UK adventure began.

CHAPTER 2

The Liverpool Years

'When I started my schooling, I found myself in a world of knowledge that was similar to the Renaissance, and when I moved to the University of Liverpool I found myself all of a sudden in the heart of the Industrial Revolution.'

Mohamed Makiya arrived in Britain in November 1935. For both Britain and Iraq, the 1930s were a decade of contrasts. There was prosperity, and new gadgets were continually coming onto the market; but there was also poverty, characterised by lines of unemployed men and rows of shabby housing.

Worst hit in the UK were the areas of heavy industry (e.g., coal, iron, steel and shipbuilding) in Northern Ireland, Scotland, Wales and the north of England. These industries were already struggling, because they had not modernised after the war and had been badly impacted by competition from other countries. But for other industries it was a time of prosperity. The motor-car industry entered its golden age, and Morris, Humber and Austin became household names in Britain. By 1934 the economy was running a healthy £31 million surplus, and taxes were cut. 'We have finished the story of *Bleak House*,' the Prime Minister Neville Chamberlain told the Commons, in April 1933 'and are sitting down this afternoon to the first chapter of *Great Expectations*.'

'Great expectations' captured Mohamed's sentiments as well when he arrived in London at the age of twenty-one with little knowledge of English. When he left, eleven years later, he would have lived through the challenging years of the Second World War and survived German bombings, and he would be the first Iraqi to hold a PhD in architecture.

❧

The electric lights and indoor plumbing of West London's fashionable Bayswater district now replaced the oil lamps and open sewers of Old Baghdad in Mohamed's life. He soon recovered from the culture shock and spent a year learning English and preparing for the entrance exam for the northern universities (Liverpool and Manchester).

From his Bayswater residence, Mohamed moved to nearby Edgware Road, also in West London. He subsequently moved one more time, this time to Finsbury Park in north London, away from the other Iraqi students – whom he avoided mixing with in order to improve his English language skills. The cheaper rent enabled him to invest in books and cultural activities. From Finsbury Park he could take a 73 bus to the Royal Polytechnic Institution (now the University of Westminster) in central London.

Finsbury Park was a middle-class suburb of two- and three-storey terrace housing that had been created in the 1860s, and whose householders, like the family Mohamed lived with, frequently rented out rooms to get by. New transport links improved Finsbury Park's appeal to commuters in the early twentieth century: the Great Northern and City Railway arrived from Moorgate in 1904, and two years later Finsbury Park became the northern terminus of the Great Northern, Piccadilly and Brompton Railway (now the Piccadilly Underground line). Edward A. Stone's art deco Astoria Cinema opened there in 1930, with an ornate interior that created the impression of a Moorish settlement at night.

Once Mohamed took a woman who also rented a room in the house to the cinema; because of this, he fell out with another lodger, who called him a 'dirty Arab'. The great age of cinema-going in Britain was the 1930s, when most people went at least once and sometimes twice a week. Early films were black-and-white, but in the 1930s the first colour films were shown. Mohamed loved the cinema, and watching films helped him improve his English.

In London he visited the cinema not only in order to learn the language, but to familiarise himself with the social mores of the English. At that time his allowance from the Iraqi government was what he called 'the princely sum' of £14 ($17) per month – which actually meant that he was well off by comparison with the other Iraqi students.

Among his Iraqi friends in the UK were Abdul Rahman al-Bazzaz, who served as the dean of the Baghdad Law College and later as the first civilian Prime Minister of Iraq in the 1960s, only to meet a gruesome death in 1968 under the ruling Baath Party's reign of terror; Saleh Mahdi Haider, who designed the Jaffariyya Secondary Schools; Hassan Dujailli, who had written a history of Baghdad University; and Ja'far Allawi, who would become one of Iraq's most prominent architects. Al-Bazzaz was called 'the priest' by his friends, as he was a strict Muslim who wanted to make sure that all his food was pork-free when he went to a restaurant. Dujailli helped Mohamed study the history of England by going through past exam papers in an attempt to anticipate the exam questions. For the translation section of the exam, Mohamed chose some verses from the Qur'an along with some literary texts. His secondary school studies in Baghdad had given him a good background in most subjects; he achieved a distinction in humanities and did well in science.

In an interview with Maureen Kubba, author of his uncompleted biography, Mohamed recalled that he 'tried, unsuccessfully, to lie about my age and make myself as old as possible so that I could go to university without having to take an English exam. I excelled in mathematics, but had to take the Wesley College Oxford Student English correspondence course for extra study.' When he took the Liverpool University entrance exam, his composition dealt with a conversation between himself and a camel. He tried to draw the attention of the examiners to what it was like living in exile, comparing himself to the camel, and quoting a poem by the pre-Islamic poet Imru al-Qais, who wrote that 'each stranger is related to every other stranger'.

When the letter arrived with the results of his exams, Mohamed was afraid to open it and asked his friend Ja'far Allawi to see if he had passed. 'Mohamed, you have done it!' Allawi exclaimed. Mohamed quickly left London for the Merseyside port city.

❦

Liverpool University had the oldest school of architecture in the UK. Writing in its own magazine, *Insight*, the late David Thistlewood, professor of the history of art and architecture there, said that to reflect on the history of the School of Architecture was to discover a microcosm of twentieth-century British architectural influences and values.

Mohamed studied in the school built specifically for the study of architecture, which had been completed in 1933. The building forms an extension to one of the Georgian houses on Abercromby Square, and is itself a modernist construction. The close attention that its architect, Sir Charles Reilly, paid to achieving harmony between the old and the new may have influenced Mohamed and helped him to develop his own philosophy about the need for a synthesis of traditional and modern architecture. Mark Crinson, author of *Modern Architecture and the End of Empire*, points out that

> [W]hen Makiya left for Liverpool he had no knowledge of indigenous Middle Eastern architecture, indeed his own interest in the regional variations of Islamic architecture dates from the measured-drawing exercises set at Liverpool.* Liverpool's training made no particular concession to its foreign students;

---

* A measured drawing is when a student of architecture visits a building, say an ancient church, and takes the measurements himself on the basis of which he then fully describes the building in drawings (plans, elevations and sections).

it was thought to have universal relevance whatever background students came from and wherever they might practise. So Mohamed studied church design and chose a recreation centre for Antibes [in France] as his final-year project. Whilst the classical pedagogy taught him design discipline, Liverpool's measuring and drawing exercises showed Mohamed how to look at historic buildings and how to appreciate variations in vernacular architecture. ... Later, when [Makiya] returned to Baghdad and established the School of Architecture at Baghdad University in 1959, he set the same kind of measured drawing work for his Iraqi students, though his aim seems to have been to foster urban conservation and an Arab identity in contemporary architecture, free of foreign influences but adjusted to contemporary needs.'[1]

We might also mention Harold Mason, who had himself been a student at the Liverpool School of Architecture. Mason had held the job of government architect in Iraq during the time of the British mandate. Along with James Wilson, he designed all major government buildings in Iraq until 1935. Mason took an interest in the students from the Middle East at the School of Architecture and had advised Mohamed to study architecture. Mason did not want to ignore indigenous architecture, and this could have influenced Mohamed.

At first the lecturers in Liverpool were not convinced that a boy from Baghdad would be able to master the subtleties of Christopher Wren and Inigo Jones.[2] One of his lecturers asked him sarcastically, 'Do you think in Arabic or in English?' Mohamed was determined to prove, both to himself and to his professors, that he could master English. He assumed the comment cast doubt on his ability to achieve that. He had a fierce belief in himself and was determined not only to succeed but to be the best. At the end of his second year in Liverpool he was among the top students in his design class. He spent his holidays cycling through the English countryside and drawing the elevations of churches and city streets.

There were many Arab students in Liverpool with whom Mohamed was friendly: engineering students like Ja'far Allawi and Midhat Ali Madloum. But while in Liverpool he did not often go to social gatherings organised by Arabs, both because he wanted to use and improve his English and because he missed the art galleries and cultural life of London. Liverpool was a poor city and, whenever he could, Mohamed would take the train to London for ten shillings (half a pound). The Iraqi government now paid him a living allowance of £16 ($22) a month – enough to live well, but not extravagantly. Peter's Pub on Egerton Street, in Liverpool, was one of his favourite haunts. His English friends called him Micky.

❧

Mohamed continued to excel in his studies. He received top marks for a design of a church that greatly impressed William Arthur Eden, an honorary lecturer in rural planning who shared his articles and books with his young student. The assignment gave Mohamed the chance to spend long hours in the university library looking through issues of architectural magazines; he eventually found a journal devoted to the design of churches in villages and towns. Describing the findings of his research to Rashid al-Khayoun, Mohamed noted that 'the church has a tower, and it gives the village a vertical dimension and breaks the monotony of horizontal houses. There is no difference between this and the minaret of a mosque in an Islamic village or city.'[3]

During the summer of 1939, Mohamed went with Professor Eden to the Cotswold market town of Chipping Campden to do measured work in a very traditionally English setting. He revelled in this opportunity, as he had always been attuned to geography, which he had been prevented from studying by a teacher at his first school – one who hadn't liked his drawings. He was so successful in his endeavours now that he went on to win a mention from another lecturer, Lionel Budden, for his design of a church.

Budden, the head of the Department of Architecture, was one of Mohamed's favourite professors. He was among the school's most renowned figures, having graduated with a BA in 1909 and an MA in 1910, beginning teaching in 1911, and becoming Associate Professor in 1924. Budden loved his students and kept in touch with some of them after they graduated. Mohamed had fond memories of going to a fancy dress party where Budden dressed as Napoleon while he came in traditional Arab clothes.

Budden wrote an exam question asking students to comment on the statement 'The house is a machine for living.' Mohamed, who got top marks in the exam, was uneasy about a purely utilitarian view of a house. Discussing his answer to the exam question with al-Khayoun, he observed that 'it reflected my view that a house provides space, tranquillity, charm, and peace, for its inhabitants.' During his studies before the outbreak of the Second World War in 1939, Mohamed began to explore the human dimension in architecture, which would be a continuing theme and preoccupation in his future work.

Mohamed recalled these days as full of learning and fun, when he wholeheartedly entered into the life of the school. He was sworn into the Students' Union during a ceremony at which he was 'knighted' with a T-square.

꙰

Mohamed was in his third year of studies at Liverpool University when the Second World War began. For a few weeks in 1940, Iraq briefly became an ally of Germany against the British, who soon regained control. Strong Iraqi anti-Anglo and anti-Semitic sentiment had already been fuelled by the German Nazi influence. Anti-British and anti-Semitic feelings were easy to stir in Iraq, because most of the Iraqi people had strong feelings about developments in Palestine – where, in 1939, the British put down Arab forces in revolt against growing Jewish influence in the region. And there was strong resentment of British rule in Iraq.

During the war, architecture students in Liverpool and the Architectural Association* became politicised, and more of them were demanding that their projects have some social relevance. It was not modernism per se – or the so-called International Style – that was being clamoured for, but rather a *socially directed* modernism.

The war years were particularly difficult for the citizens of Liverpool. Documenting the destruction during the Blitz, the Merseyside Maritime Museum noted that Liverpool was the most heavily bombed British city outside of London. It was a prime target for attack because, along with Birkenhead, its 'twin' across the Mersey, it was the country's biggest West Coast port. The city was a lifeline for Britain's maritime trade, being the main point of entry for imported fuel, food and raw materials; ships arrived every week.

The fall of Norway, Holland, Belgium and France to the German army by mid-1940 allowed the Luftwaffe to use airfields in each of those countries to bomb Merseyside. The German air raids of 1940–42 caused death and destruction on both sides of the Mersey: about 4,000 people were killed, including 2,736 in Liverpool, 454 in Birkenhead, and 424 in Bootle.

In Liverpool, many docks and their neighbourhoods were reduced to rubble. Much of the city centre was devastated, including the main shopping and business areas. Some of the city's best-known buildings were destroyed, including the Customs House, the Cotton Exchange, the Rotunda Theatre, and Lewis's department store. The City Museum (now the World Museum) and Central Library, along with their fine collections, were also badly damaged. A number of ships were sunk in the docks and the river.

But apart from a German bomb raid on Merseyside on 13 March 1941, the university managed to escape the devastation. The corner

---

* The Architectural Association was founded in London in 1847 by a group of young articled pupils as a reaction against the prevailing conditions under which architectural training could be obtained. By the late 1930s, the Association had become home to radical ideas of the Left and the UK's first modernist school.

portion of its engineering laboratory was severely damaged by a bomb, as were the medical school and the pathology and physiology laboratories. The only people on duty were the members of the Auxiliary Fire Service (AFS) and fire-fighting services, and no one was seriously injured; a night watchman was slightly cut by flying glass.

Most of the British students who began their studies with Mohamed interrupted them to join the armed forces. When war broke out, there were only a few students left: a Chinese, Zhanxiang; a Turk; two Egyptians; one British conscientious objector; and Mohamed himself, the sole Iraqi. The female students took up jobs in civil defence or as medics; a farewell party was held for the male students before they left to join the army. Mohamed was very much affected when one of his British friends was subsequently killed in combat.

Mohamed remembered being assigned to fire-watching duties, and he recalled how these young men mostly took in their stride the shrapnel flying over their heads, the bombing, and the fires, hiding under staircases rather than resorting to the shelters. When the bombs were falling on Liverpool, the students took refuge in the basement, where they spent many nights. It was a time of food rationing; the typical weekly ration was three pints of milk, one egg, 50g of tea and 225g of sugar. Every four weeks, 350g of sweets were allowed. The Yemeni students at the university hosted a lavish party to celebrate the Eid al-Fitr religious holiday marking the end of Ramadan. They managed to circumvent the meat ration of half a pound (225g) per person on the pretext of religious observance, and acquired a whole sheep. Mohamed kept a dried orange skin as a memento of those days of rationing.

Mohamed did manage a trip to London in the autumn of 1940 and had a wonderful time despite the German V1 and V2 raids. He was able to go to the theatre.

When he visited China forty years after the war, Mohamed was received at the airport by his former classmate Zhanxiang: Mohamed was a member of the steering committee for the Aga Khan Awards for Architecture, and Zhanxiang and Mohamed spent a pleasant evening reminiscing about their student days.

Mohamed's final project in Liverpool was connected with the rebuilding of the city, whose destruction he had witnessed first-hand. He first thought about submitting a design for a tourist resort in Kurdistan, but the Iraqi government regarded maps of the region as military secrets, and there were few resources for him to utilise. He settled instead on Liverpool and produced a drawing: 'Reconstruction of Central Liverpool – Church Street Waterloo Place' to complete the project.

❧

When war had broken out the Iraqi government had decided that Iraqi students on scholarships in Britain should return home.* The Iraqi embassy instructed them to go to a safe area away from the bombs, so a brief interlude in Bangor, a quaint Welsh port city with a population of 18,000, followed. (The Iraqi embassy's choice of Bangor may have been inspired by the BBC's decision to move its Light Entertainment department to Bangor, one of the smallest cities in Britain, with a university established in 1885).

At first the Iraqi student 'refugees' enjoyed themselves, discussing politics and sightseeing. They were waiting for the government of Iraq to send a ship that would take them home via Beirut or some other port. But the promised ship never arrived, and there was little for the students to do apart from talking about politics and engaging in fiery debates in cafés and pubs – which started to annoy the locals, who did not appreciate heated discussions in a language they did not understand.

---

* Forty-five Iraqi students came to study in Britain in 1935.

Mohamed graduated with a Bachelor of Architecture in 1941. The thought of continuing his studies at Harvard University crossed his mind, but one of his lecturers, who was also his friend, persuaded him that the German army, which was already in France, would soon be defeated and the war would be over. Mohamed changed his mind and spent another year in Liverpool, studying for a post-graduate degree in Civic Design. Shortly thereafter, Mohamed was accepted in the doctoral programme at King's College in Cambridge.

In 1942 Mohamed met his future wife, Margaret Crawford, at Liverpool University's annual party. Before enrolling for a teacher-training course she studied European and British medieval history and received a prize for her dissertation on the history of philosophy.

CHAPTER 3

The Cambridge Years

'I was lucky enough to study for a PhD at King's College in Cambridge, where the only thing I did was go to the library. There was no professor who could tell me anything about Islamic architecture there, so they left me free.'

Both Mohamed and Margaret, his future wife, were excellent students. In Cambridge Mohamed studied for his PhD and Margaret enrolled for a teacher-training course at a private college. Her father was a strict headmaster in New Mills, Derbyshire, and he held both Margaret and her brother, Alan, to a strict disciplinary regime. Even when Margaret was in her twenties, she had to go to sleep at 9 p.m., and 'lights out' was imposed as if she were in boarding school.

For a number of years Margaret kept her relationship with Mohamed secret. In the 1930s it was not uncommon for Arabs to be referred to as 'towelheads', and discrimination was rife; bars put up signs saying 'No Arabs allowed'. Margaret's family adhered to these views, and Margaret paid the price. In the end she was forced to make a choice, and she simply broke with her past and cut all ties with her family. But whereas Margaret's family disapproved of the relationship, Mohamed's family loved and respected her.

At first it was not clear whether the Iraqi government would continue to finance Mohamed's studies. A contractor named Umran Tawfik, who was from the same neighbourhood in Baghdad as Mohamed, agreed to help him if the need arose. But the funding of Mohamed's studies was discussed in Parliament, and the government agreed to cover all his costs.¹ The Iraqi Minister of Education, an almost permanent member of the Iraqi Parliament in the first half of the twentieth century, played a major role in securing a further scholarship for Mohamed.

When Mohamed was applying for admission to Cambridge, economics professor Edward Shaw asked him two questions: Why do you want to study at King's College in Cambridge? and: Who is financing you? Mohamed replied that the traditions and history of Cambridge were very much like those of Najaf in southern Iraq, a city of Shi'i learning, and he wanted to study in a university town in England. King's College Cambridge was founded in 1441 by Henry VI. The chapel, which was begun in 1446 by Henry VI and took over a century to build, is a splendid example of late Gothic (perpendicular) architecture. It boasts the world's largest fan vault (a form used in the Gothic style, in which the ribs are all of the same curve), and some of the finest medieval stained glass.

Mohamed was enchanted by the view of the curving river, with its feathery trees in beautiful rounded shapes, the spreading lawns, and the pearly white buildings of the colleges, one behind the other. During the war, Cambridge was subject to the usual air-raid precautions and blackouts along with the shortages that affected the whole country, but damage was negligible. (It was commonly believed that the German air force refrained from bombing Cambridge because they thought this would deter the RAF from bombing Heidelberg.) Teaching continued throughout the war years, even though the Home Guard and civil defence made heavy demands on the staff. In 1942, of 370 lecturers and practical teachers only 143 remained in Cambridge.*

As the war intensified, many of the young men were called away from Cambridge to fulfil roles for which they had been earmarked

---

* By 1942–43 the university had developed a scheme which allowed men to come up to Cambridge as cadets and study for two terms while doing their military training. This period of residence and the passing of a cadet's examination would contribute to a 'war degree' if they returned after service.

earlier. Those left behind in college helped the war effort in the early days by fire-watching from the chapel roof and trench-digging outside the choir school. One zigzag trench was intended to serve as an air raid shelter.

Soon after the declaration of war, the principal of Queen Mary College, London, shrewdly evacuated his college to the relative safety of the 'countryside', in the guise of King's College. In addition to the fifty or so students from Queen Mary, King's housed between 100 and 170 of its own students during the first years of the war.

❧❦

During his time at Cambridge Mohamed enjoyed the debates at the Students' Union, which he likened to parliamentary debates. He debated the fate of the Eastern Mediterranean and the establishment of the State of Israel: his view was that the cruelty that had been done to the Jews was a heinous crime, but that the price of changing geography would be long-lasting. He wrote an article on Jewish settlement that was published in the *Town Planning Review*, pointing out that Jerusalem and the Dome of the Rock were sacred to all religions and not just one faith. He won the debate.

During his years in Cambridge (1943–46), Mohamed focused on his dissertation, which dealt with the influence of climate on architectural development in the Mediterranean region. He took advantage of the opportunity that Cambridge offered to broaden his horizons – attending lectures delivered by eminent professors on a variety of subjects. He heard Bertrand Russell lecture on philosophy, and Eric Newton on fine art, and sat on the floor at the crowded lectures on political history by Harold Laski of the London School of Economics and Political Science (LSE).

Mohamed was impressed with one of the distinguished professors, George Trevelyan, and his book *English Social History: A Survey of Six Centuries*, which told history through the story of creative people rather than powerful rulers. But the professor he felt closest to was Albert Edward Richardson, an authority on classic architecture, who included a chapter on Islamic buildings in his book *The Art of Architecture*. Mohamed was the only non-arts student to attend a series of talks by Eric Newton on the history of European art. And to compensate for his not being able to study geography in Iraq, he went to lectures given by Professor Dudley Stamp.

In Cambridge, the Dorothy Café near the river was a favourite haunt. Ships were carved into the outside walls of the building. The British philosopher, logician and social reformer Bertrand Russell sometimes joined students there. Mohamed was taken by his unassuming, humble nature and later corresponded with Russell about a private Shi'i university he dreamed of establishing in Iraq when he returned home after completing his studies.

※

His spare time was spent with Margaret, and much of what little money they had between them went on books. The couple enjoyed a full social life with friends and attended cultural events.

Mohamed's brother Abdul Aziz, who became a doctor and opened his own practice in Baghdad, sent Mohamed his share of the money realised from the sale of the family home. These funds helped Mohamed and Margaret finance their frequent trips to the English countryside. But Mohamed subsequently very much regretted the sale of the house and tried unsuccessfully to buy it back.

Mohamed's Cambridge days, when he was writing his PhD dissertation, were also the days of long bicycle rides through rural England with Margaret. They explored splendid market towns and villages of honey-coloured stone. They visited some of England's greatest palaces and country houses, and some of the most famous arboreta in Britain. They marvelled at the natural world, taking in breathtaking landscapes and acclaimed nature reserves. They cycled and walked along historic trails. In the Cotswold towns of Cheltenham, Cirencester, Gloucester, Tewkesbury and Stroud, they went to local markets and fairs, bought old books, and delighted in a wealth of cultural and crafts festivals. They stayed in charming B&Bs. They even went as far as Scotland on their bikes. They were young and in love as they planned their future life.

Margaret qualified as a teacher and took a job in Ely, a historic Cathedral town fourteen miles from Cambridge. They were together on weekends, when Margaret visited Mohamed with her favourite dog. He remembered a letter she sent saying that the dog had left one day and never returned, which reminded him of the lamb he had befriended in Baghdad.

Even though Mohamed did not like writing, he never failed to correspond with his family in Baghdad. His niece Amal recalled, 'Mohamed sent postcards to my father with photos of England, to let him see the views and the buildings.'

Mohamed's daughter, Hind, recalled her father's difficulties in writing: 'When Dad was doing his PhD in Cambridge he had lots of ideas. He had a brilliant mind when it came to architecture, but a terrible memory. Mum translated his ideas into academic English, and she kept correcting his writing. He was a terrible writer.' Margaret would subsequently edit his articles until the 1970s, after which Hind and her brother, Kanan, took on that responsibility. His colleague Diddi Malek helped write his speech to the Royal Institute of British Architects. (*Arab architecture past and present* – see Appendix 2).

৵৽৶

Initially, Mohamed wanted to write his PhD dissertation about Israeli settlements on the al-Assi River in Lebanon. He objected to these settlements, not just because they were built on confiscated land, but also as they were imported settlements at odds with the traditional buildings in the area. But he gave up on this idea and instead produced a dissertation with the title 'Architecture and the Mediterranean Climate: Studies on the Effect of Climatic Conditions on Architectural

Development in the Mediterranean Region with Special Reference to the Prospects of Its Practice in the "Near East"'.

Professor A. W. Lawrence, the brother of T. E. Lawrence, the controversial figure known as Lawrence of Arabia, was one of the examiners of Mohamed's PhD dissertation. He specialised in classic studies of the history of Greek and Roman art in the Mediterranean. In the abstract to his dissertation, Mohamed argued that 'if architecture is to be an art exercising a positive influence towards the good, then an attempt must be made to discuss its relevance to the ethical values of society, traditional values of time and the cultural values of space: these three considerations make up the fundamental basis of its comprehensive scholarly understanding needed in the face of present chaotic mannerisms'.

This philosophy, with its emphasis on what Mohamed called 'the human scale', was the guiding principle underlying all his future work. He emphasised that everything has to be brought back to the human being, a person's relationship with other human beings, to society and nature and the environment. This was the theme of his thesis submitted to Cambridge University. In his later work he tried to expand this theory.

Mohamed's philosophy of architecture was also very strongly influenced by his Islamic belief. He discussed this with al-Khayoun when he said that: 'The relationship to the environment and the universe is one of harmony. This is what our Islamic belief and heritage teaches us. It is a record of past achievements and provides a guide for the future. It contains the morals and spiritual heritage of our nation.' Mohamed considered the Qur'an and the Bible as the sources of his dissertation, as 'both books refer to the geographical theatre which is the topic of my study. Many verses talk about place and what is related to it especially in the Mediterranean environment.'

The back cover of a publication titled *Environmental Design Studies and Practice in Arab Countries* quotes Mohamed as saying 'Islamic philosophy is based on humanism, and the theory of "oneness" or "unity, tawhid in Arabic". Every man is a member of the universe, past, present and future, not just a member of the present. Through this, man is integrated into a "oneness" with his environment.'

Mohamed also spoke about the responsibility that architects carry, given that their work is long-lasting, taking up space on the ground and in the sky.

༄༅

Much of Mohamed's time in Cambridge was spent in the library: 'I would often be forgotten by the library staff and locked in over lunchtime. I wished desperately that I could own all the books I touched. I knew I was obliged to return to Iraq, and I did not want to leave such treasures behind.'

Mohamed had spent one year in the civic design department at Liverpool University, the only such department in England. He was influenced by John Ruskin, the art and architecture critic and writer who believed that a building reached its prime after five centuries and ought to be designed with this in mind. Mohamed had learned from English architects (Christopher Wren, Inigo Jones) the way to do measured work. The idea at the time was to measure something classical, like a Georgian house or a Greek column, as an exercise in design and craftsmanship. Makiya instead asked: why not work in the laboratory of nature and God?

After graduation, and receiving his doctorate in architecture from King's College in 1946, Mohamed wanted to stay in England. 'I lived in England during the time before the war, through the war and after the war. I had not been outside the circle of danger; at any time a missile could have hit the student accommodations. I lost friends who went to the front and did not come back.'[2]

The money from the sale of the family home in Iraq continued to finance his trips to the shires as well as a trip to Ireland with Margaret, now his fiancée. They were still visiting antiques markets and buying rare books.

He was invited to London University to give a talk on 'The Influence of Western Civilisation on Arab Art and the Arab Environment', as part of the festivities of Arab week, held in 1946. After the lecture, the dean of the university invited him to a dinner for Arab ambassadors. Mohamed was happy to attend but refused to shake hands with Prince Abd al-Ilah, the regent of Iraq. He believed that this 'rebellious act' affected his career when he returned home, because the architectural firm that he established did not get any major contracts for some years.

The journey home for Mohamed was very different from the journey to Britain. He returned by plane, via Rome and Cairo; he stayed in Cairo for ten days in a hotel where only French or English was spoken, not Arabic, and where all the waiters were Greek. He was very eager to see the Fatimid capital city,* which was once the vanguard of Islamic thought and a point of contact between the Arab world and the civilisations of the Mediterranean, and he visited the Islamic Museum, the Catholic Museum, the pyramids and Al-Azhar University.

He saw the mosques of al-Hussein and Ibn Tulun, being especially impressed by the latter, a testament to Iraqi influence on Mediterranean culture. He was also intrigued by the two beautiful houses that an Englishman had combined to convey a feeling of a traditional Cairo residence. Before leaving Cairo, a city he had hitherto seen only in photographs and book illustrations, he scoured antique shops and bought tiles from Fatimid times.

Mohamed reached Baghdad happy and proud of his antiques, but not everyone shared his enthusiasm. One of the first things his brother asked was: 'What are these relics?'

---

* The Fatimid dynasty first established itself in Tunisia in December 303 AH/909 AD. In order to expand their realm and to make it more effective, the Fatimids needed a capital more central than Tunisia. Egypt – a convenient centre for Syria, Palestine, Arabia and the Mediterranean Islands – presented excellent possibilities. Thus, the Fatimids conquered Egypt and built the city of al-Qahirah (Cairo) to be their new capital.

CHAPTER 4

Return to Iraq

*'When I left Iraq, it was in the Middle Ages.
When I came back, it was in the modern age.'*

Mohamed left Baghdad in 1935 breathless with excitement; he returned in 1946 in the same frame of mind. But it was a different kind of excitement this time. When the small plane landed, his family, friends and relatives were there to greet him. 'I saw the big gathering in the distance, with my mother in front and my maternal uncle Aboud and brother, Abdul Aziz. They managed to get into the restricted area. When the plane's doors opened, my brother rushed toward me,' Mohamed recalled when talking to Rashid al-Khayoun. 'My mother was waiting in the reception area. She could not speak, because she was crying. She saw me as still a child, in need of her care and attention. I was not at all surprised that she took a ripe pear out of her pocket and put it into my hand when we were on the way home. The way she smuggled the pear from her pocket into my hand reminded me of my youth, when my mother would give me and my brother food out of sight of my half-brothers and their wives. Maybe she did not want to embarrass me in front of other people, as I was returning with a higher degree from my studies.'[1]

But Mohamed had changed, and Baghdad had changed. He noticed that the date palms were still in front of the houses, but new houses had supplanted a flower garden where he used to spend time, and the land had been divided into plots. Before Margaret's arrival, Mohamed lived with his brother in eastern Karada in the Abu Qlam district in central Baghdad. Many of his acquaintances from the

Sabbabigh al-Aal district where he grew up were now in Abu Qlam. It worried him that the area had been denuded of its farmland, and only one small farm was left by the road. There were obligatory visits to all who had assisted him in getting the scholarship to Britain, including Minister Sadiq al-Bassam. Everyone was proud of him, as he was from the first generation of Shi'i residents to study abroad.

The Baghdad that Mohamed Makiya returned to in 1946 had been transformed by British influence. In the 1950s, a Red Crescent Fashion Show held in al-Amana hall featured elegant models in floral-print summer dresses – a total contrast to the traditional black *abayas* of the 1930s. Baghdad was modernising: it had become a city of paved roads linked to the rest of the world by regular rail and air services.

By the 1940s al-Rashid Street was the place to go for late-night entertainment, with thirty nightclubs, twenty cinemas and nine theatres along its two-kilometre length. Baghdad's best-known cafés were on this street: the Umm Kulthum, named after the Egyptian diva whose music they played, and al-Zahawi, named after a poet and philosopher. A favoured haunt of artists, students and the intelligentsia and a hotbed for the recruitment of political activists, al-Rashid Street had become the Mesopotamian equivalent of what the Parisian Left Bank would become in the 1950s.

In 1955 Iraq signed a mutual defence treaty with Turkey; the UK, Pakistan and Iran were later signatories. The British-installed monarchy faced increasing resentment from Iraqis, and this 'Baghdad Pact' did not enjoy support from the greater populace. This discontent culminated in a major uprising in 1948, when the Portsmouth Treaty was initiated, proposing a board of Iraqis and British representatives to decide on defence matters of mutual interest. The treaty was withdrawn.

The dominant political figure of this era was Nuri al-Said, whose career encompassed forty-seven cabinet posts. During one of his stints as Prime Minister he suspended the publication of newspapers, enforced a curfew, and imposed a ban on all political parties, characterising them as mainly opportunist bodies. Meanwhile inflation rose, poverty deepened, slums proliferated and corruption became rife, while the elite prospered.

❧❧

Mohamed's first job when he returned to Iraq from London was a part-time lectureship at the school of engineering at Baghdad University. Finding a permanent position that would utilise his skills and qualifications proved a challenge. He was dismayed at the attitude of the head of the planning council, Arshad al-Umari, who asked him why a PhD was necessary in a country like Iraq, and in fact forced the Minister of Education to cancel PhD scholarships going forward.

In 1947 Mohamed joined the Directorate General of Municipalities in Baghdad as an architect and town planner. During his six years with the directorate, he introduced the concept of town planning and set up the first surveys and proposals for replanning towns throughout Iraq. He discovered that al-Umari was responsible for dividing agricultural land into small plots (300 sq. metres to 6,000 sq. metres). By making it a planning condition that a house should be no more than four metres away from a fence, the law, with the stroke of a pen, had destroyed the idea of having the traditional internal courtyard. Al-Umari had also allowed the extension of al-Rashid Street by demolishing part of the Marjan mosque, one of Baghdad's landmarks.

Mohamed soon discovered that, despite its impressive-sounding name, the Directorate General of Municipalities was little more than an office for keeping copies of maps and acting as a consultancy to decision makers. But the Directorate could not enforce the implementation of its recommendations. Mohamed felt that planning ought to be the responsibility of local councils in Iraq's governorates, who could implement decisions.

He travelled extensively around Iraq during his first years back, and tried to do something about the lack of maps of the country's various regions. But the Ministry of Defence had decreed that maps were top secret. Mohamed sent for maps from the British Royal Air Force in Cairo and received a number of aerial photographs, including photos of Erbil. He wondered how the maps could be confidential if the British were printing them.

While he served in the Directorate General of Municipalities, most of Mohamed's suggestions fell on deaf ears. He proposed the development of a green belt around Baghdad and a botanical garden and zoo on the Isle of Pigs, an island in the Tigris south of Baghdad. The suggestion for the green belt incurred the wrath of the Ministry of Works and Irrigation and the Interior Ministry. The latter saw it as taking away land for urban development to no useful purpose.

At the same time, Mohamed directed his efforts towards empowering the Directorate General of Municipalities in Baghdad by making it independent of the governors of the provinces and of the Interior Ministry, in particular where decisions about preserving the country's traditional fabric were concerned. He was worried that roads were arbitrarily built criss-crossing the holy cities of Najaf and Karbala, violating their holy spaces and buildings. In Najaf, the city wall was demolished in an ill-fated effort to solve the problem of population density. Mohamed thought that the inner core of the traditional city of Najaf should have been surrounded by a 'green belt' of date palms. He advocated the formation of cooperatives, backed by local banks, to finance development projects, and produced numerous reports documenting the destruction of the country's heritage; he reportedly put forward suggestions for its preservation. Sadly, the Directorate had no power to implement his suggestions.

Mohamed was never happy working for the Directorate and was looking for an excuse to submit his resignation. One day in 1951 a minister came to the office, and when he discovered Mohamed was not there, made a complaint in Parliament. It was the last straw, and Mohamed's life as a man running his own full-time architectural practice began.

School of Architecture, Liverpool University (Pic: Iain Jackson)

Makiya Associates Baghdad Office. (© Mohamed Makiya Archive, courtesy of Aga Khan Documentation Center, MIT Libraries – AKDC@MIT)

In later years, reflecting on his government job, Mohamed observed to friends: 'I was told, in no uncertain terms, that I was too highly qualified and that my philosophising was a threat to the smooth running of local government. The Baghdad of my youth – the Tigris, the stars, the sky and the palm trees – was growing along thoroughfares that had been cut through its heart with no appreciation of, or connection to, the river.'

☙❧

Makiya Associates had been established in 1946 when Mohamed first returned to Iraq, with a clear vision of how he intended to work. After leaving the Directorate he worked as head of the firm until it closed in 1988.

A brochure introducing Makiya Associates described it as a private architectural and planning practice. 'The buildings and projects designed by the office are located in the Arab countries of the Middle East. This geographical location implies a specific cultural, social and climatic environment. An architectural practice cannot isolate itself from such influences. Naturally there are many other forces affecting both the internal design of buildings and their relationship to each other. For example, contemporary buildings are built out of new and modern building materials and technological systems.' The brochure went on to note that 'modern buildings also have to fulfil modern functions which have standard requirements that apply internationally, regardless of location. Although modern technology and user requirements are implicit in the solution of any design problem, nevertheless the particular environment has its own overriding influence on the final design. If this were not the case, then were would be no reason for having architects and planners. Government buildings, office blocks and housing complexes could be duplicated from the best examples taken from other parts of the world.'

The philosophy expounded in Mohamed's PhD thesis was being put into practice. Makiya Associates took as its guiding method in design the spatial needs generated by a society whose religion is Islam, whose culture is Arab, and which is geographically located in a Middle Eastern climate and terrain. And, the brochure noted, the projects undertaken by Makiya Associates reflect the practical results of such an approach to architectural planning. 'It is not enough to start from the assumption that modern Arab design is a copy in the Middle East of solutions that have evolved in response to the needs of other societies. The character of the Middle Eastern environment is deeply rooted in Islam and its Arabic culture. This cannot be arrived at as an afterthought, to be added on to a design solution that is more or less complete. A modern Middle Eastern architecture involves a deeply sympathetic attitude towards the fundamental principles of space utilisation inherent in the culture of the region. It involves an appreciation of the historical tradition of Islamic-Arab architecture. We believe that such an approach cannot be imported. It can only derive from a deep and permanent attachment to the values and culture of the Arab world.'

One of the early projects Mohamed much later told the author Lawrence Weschler about was the design of a house for a judge of the Baghdad court, Sayed Hadi. 'When Mohamed did get work,' Weschler writes, 'there were no contracts, and often no detailed plans. He would have to improvise on the spot. A client frequently paid in goods, not money. Discussing [fees] in advance was considered crass. Sometimes Mohamed was compensated with carpets; once, a sheik in southern Iraq gave him a cow as payment. "And a rather nasty cow at that," Margaret recalled. "Used to kick like hell."'[2]

In the 1950s, Mohamed was more of a contractor than an architect. He dealt directly with the workers, and his projects were contracts for the construction of a whole building and the provision of building materials. Despite his lack of formal training in the contracting business he soon adapted, filling the gaps from his academic university days via hands-on experience.

Mohamed greatly respected traditional builders and developed an excellent working relationship with them. The builders-cum-architects lived in Hitawin, east of Sabbabigh al-Aal in Old Baghdad where Mohamed grew up. Most of them wore traditional Baghdadi dress: a suit consisting of a coat, a jacket, and a longer garment. One of the most famous traditional builders Mohamed employed was *Ustad* (Master) Hasan Faraj, an expert in constructing brick ceilings. Faraj worked on the Khulafa Mosque and the houses and buildings of Kazim Makiya.

In building the house of a distinguished family from Mosul, Mohamed enlisted the help of *Ustad* Hamoudi, a famous traditional builder who had built the family home that Mohamed grew up in in Sabbabigh al-Aal. Hamoudi had had no university education: building traditions and skills had been passed on from father to son. Hamoudi built the thick columns on Baghdad's famous al-Rashid Street.

In the 1950s, Mohamed built houses for Iraq's royal family, among them the house of Princess Badeea, a niece of King Faisal. His career as a contractor came to an end in the spring of 1953 with a low-cost housing project. The Tigris flooded, and the project's whole brick-making operation was washed away; tons of materials disappeared. Mohamed was held liable for the loss, and it took him a long time to recover from this disaster. But he kept on working and designing.

Mohamed's right-hand man and 'Mr Fixit' in all matters pertaining to both his household and his contracting business was a towering, one-eyed Kurd who gave the family a brown bear cub as a present. Inevitably it grew much larger and noisier and had to be chained up in the yard. Although the Kurd enjoyed coming around to wrestle with it, the decision was taken to present it to the young King as an addition to his menagerie. The Kurd found new ways of expending energy by departing to the north to take part in the resistance movement of his people. (The bear came to a sad end during the 1958 coup, when the enthusiastic revolutionaries, drunk on the ideology of liberation, naively opened the cages in the King's zoo and let out all the animals. The bear galloped down al-Rashid Street, terrified passers-by, and was shot.)

Despite the busy schedule at the office, Mohamed found time to travel. In 1951 he made the first of many trips to Cairo, as a UNESCO delegate, to present a philosophical paper on the Arab village and village industry. On subsequent visits he discovered that developments on the banks of the Nile exhibited the same lack of foresight that he had tried to legislate against in Baghdad. To Mohamed's dismay, there was no evidence of respect for the city or for the glory that was the Nile. It had become dehumanised and poverty-stricken. The human scale and the ancient backdrop had both been forgotten.

CHAPTER 5

Mohamed and Margaret in Baghdad

'The thing that was good for people in Iraq was the social life, if you had a certain level of income or educational qualifications. There were clubs rather like American country clubs: they had cinemas, swimming pools, sports, dances, and talks.'

Margaret had finally arrived in Baghdad in 1948. Always an independent woman, she obtained a contract to teach English literature at Baghdad University – a job she had applied for in the UK, responding to an advertisement in a newspaper. It was very important for her to come to Iraq as an independent and self-sufficient person.

Margaret's arrival was delayed by a cholera epidemic. To avoid coming down with the disease she stayed in Beirut for two months. Mohamed's relative Khadim, who was living in Aleppo, arranged accommodation for her and took care of her expenses.

'I remember when my auntie Margaret came to Iraq,' Mohamed's niece Amal recalled. 'I was the only one to meet her. My uncle took me with him. She came on one of the big buses from Lebanon called "Nairn", after the Scottish businessman Tom Nairn, and we met her at the bus depot.'

For Margaret, her arrival in Baghdad signalled the end of relations with her family, who cut her off completely for leaving England to marry an Arab. Mohamed's family and the Iraqi people she met, on the other hand, loved Margaret and respected the way she integrated into Iraqi society. She learned Arabic and dressed modestly in deference to Muslim customs. When she first arrived, she stayed in a hotel until the wedding.

Margaret insisted on marrying in Iraq and having a traditional Muslim wedding. After the wedding the couple rented a flat from Khadim on Mustansir Street, which provided them with a living space and an office.

'The Makiyas were members of what Iraqi people at that time called "the progressive middle class" or the "intelligentsia",' writes Nick Cohen in *What's Left? How Liberals Lost Their Way*, his 2007 book reflecting on the 2003 Iraq war. 'They brought fresh ideas with them when they settled in Baghdad. They had the self-confidence of a young, bright couple who see the future full of possibilities in front of them.'[1] They both radiated wisdom, warmth and kindness, and those who met them soon came to realise that they were a very special couple, totally devoted to one another yet both strong personalities with their own opinions. Throughout their marriage, Margaret was content for her husband to be in the limelight. She supported him in her own quiet way, editing his writing and providing a sympathetic yet critical sounding board for his ideas.

Dia Kashi, now a London resident, whose family had an antique and carpet business in Baghdad, got to know many non-Iraqi wives, including Margaret. 'They became Iraqis,' he told me. 'Mohamed and Margaret were interested in collecting antiques and fine Persian carpets. They used to come to our shop in the centre of Baghdad and we got to know them.'

Margaret immersed herself in Iraqi culture. A historian by profession, while in Iraq she became interested in the journeys foreigners made both to Iraq and to the Middle East.

Her only negative experience during the twenty-four years she spent in Iraq (1948–72) came with the Suez crisis in 1956, when demonstrators hostile to foreigners were in the streets. Dr Sadiq al-Khalili, a close friend of the family and one of the most senior professors in the College of Arts at Baghdad University where she taught, insisted that he accompanied her when she travelled by car. Her car was never attacked, and she was very grateful for his support.

Because she was a foreign employee, Margaret was given a house in the al-Alwiya district, originally built by the British to accommodate their colonial administrators. All the houses in the district were connected to the famous al-Alwiya Club, founded in 1924 by the British explorer and diplomat Gertrude Bell. This club always considered itself a place apart; its bar served English spirits but not the customary Iraqi spirit, arak. In the early years, before it opened to the Iraqi upper crust, only foreigners were allowed to become members. The club is still open today, but religious extremists condemn its free flow of alcohol.

From 1949 to 1957, the Makiyas lived in Alwiya bungalow No. 19, once occupied by the orientalist Freya Stark. Both their children were born in the bungalow, Kanan in 1949 and Hind in 1952. 'My father said that when I was born I had a cucumber head,' Hind told me. 'I had to be forced out. My eyes were shut. The muscles did not work. That's why I speak with a lisp. But I try to keep going,' she added triumphantly.[2]

Al-Alwiya district was the area where most of the British lived, in addition to Iraqis with a British spouse. Dr Doris Critchley, a doctor well known in the community, was the Makiya's neighbour in the al-Alwiya bungalow. She was very close to Margaret, and presided over the birth of her two children.

Amal recalled: 'Dr Sadiq al-Hilali had only two words for Margaret: "the best". Many Iraqi men got married to British ladies, but he said the best one was Margaret. She was teaching in the university, she was very educated, she learned Arabic – and she talked to my grandmother and to her relatives in broken Arabic, but never mind. At my wedding she sat with the old Iraqi ladies. I really loved her. She supported my uncle. She *was* the best.'

'My mother was called "the English woman who is one of us",' Hind remembered with a nostalgic tone in her voice. 'When necessary she dressed in an *abaya* [large black cloak], but she was always elegant. She had high cheekbones and wore her hair up. It wasn't curly. I got my curls from my father.'

Hind and her brother, Kanan, grew up with a Chaldean nanny, Lilly Joseph, who treated them like her own children. The nuns in the orphanage where Lilly was staying introduced her to the Makiya family, and she stayed with them until she got married; Mohamed gave her away at her wedding. She immigrated to Chicago in 1967 and worked in a canning factory. In 2005, Kanan paid for her trip to London, where she stayed for a week and was overjoyed to see Margaret, whom she adored. She still keeps in touch with Kanan.

Kanan and Hind both went to *Ta'sissiya* primary school, where the headmaster was a Mr Richard Lister. 'Both of them had just started school when the 1958 revolution broke out,' Margaret said in an interview recorded by her granddaughter, Bushra. 'That was a big blow. All the schools with a foreign element in them were under big suspicion. For a time the primary school, which was run by the British Council, was closed down, and for one term Hind went to a convent school, which had a much stricter discipline than the British Council School. But the British Council school soon opened again.'

Kanan then went to Baghdad College, an elite school for boys aged eleven to eighteen run by American Jesuits from Boston. It was comparable to Eton College in the UK and arguably Iraq's most famous secondary school for boys, having produced an Iraqi prime minister, a deputy prime minister, a vice president, two billionaires, and a member of the British House of Lords, among many other notable alumni. Hind studied at the American High School for girls. There were few secondary schools to choose from in Baghdad, and Kanan and Hind both went to the best. Their parents were very attentive to their education without being pushy, and both children were clever and conscientious.

According to Margaret (in conversation with Bushra), 'The thing that was good for people in Iraq was the social life, if you had a certain level of income or educational qualifications. There were clubs, rather like the American country clubs. They had cinemas, swimming pools, sports, dance and talks. There is quite a long, hot

Mohamed and Margaret with their children Kanan and Hind (family archive)

summer in Iraq. Both my children were good at swimming. I think they had a happy upbringing.'

The highlight of family life in Iraq was the holidays. There were many trips to archaeological sites. On a visit to Hatra, a large ancient city built in the first century CE, Kanan, Hind and their friends pretended they were archaeologists running around the ruins and living in the same huts as Professor David Oates and his wife, Joan, who specialised in the Ancient Near East. Professor Oates was director of excavations in Nimrud from 1958 to 1962. It was in Hatra that Kanan met his future wife, Wallada. They lost touch after he left Iraq in 1968 but reconnected when he returned in 2003, and their love story had a fairy-tale ending when they married in 2005.

There were also trips to Iraqi Kurdistan in the north and to the marshes of southern Iraq. It was here that the Ma'dan (marsh Arabs) built their legendary ancient civilisation, famous for its floating reed huts and boats, dating back to Sumerian times, 6,000 years ago. Kanan was especially fond of Amadiya, a 4,000-year-old town dating from the Assyrian period, located atop a mountain plateau with stunning views of the surrounding mountains and valleys.

Like thousands of Iraqis, the Makiyas fled from the oppressive heat of the Baghdad summer to the pleasant mild climate of the north, where the scenery is magnificent: sometimes wooded and watered by turbulent streams, sometimes gaunt and bare, but always dramatic. They would complete the journey to their holiday retreat on mules. On one occasion they spent a couple of months among the Kurdish people, whom they loved and respected.

In a video interview with her grandson, Naseem, Margaret reminisced that the journeys to the north and the south were her happiest times during her twenty-four years in Iraq. 'We went to one of the small resort towns in the Kurdish area, and we hired mules and took the mules as high up as they would take us, until we reached the place where you could look to Turkey and to Iran but you were still in Iraq. That is really one of my strong, vivid memories. I consider it was really a privilege to have made that journey,' Margaret recalled.

She also told Naseem about a journey the family made to Basra in the south of Iraq. At that time there was a large area of marshlands where the marsh Arabs had their own unique culture. It was also a sanctuary for birds. The birds came for a certain period and then moved on again. The storks usually return to the same nest on top of the roof of a small dome of a mosque.

'I remember the journey we made to the south was at the time of the year when the marshes were covered with a flower that was growing on top of water. The stillness and beauty of the area is something really unforgettable,' Margaret said.*

---

* In 2013 the marshlands were declared Iraq's first national park; in June 2016 they were declared a UNESCO World Heritage Site. They once stretched across some 20,000 square kilometres (7,700 square miles), but they were devastated after Saddam Hussein's horrendous drainage programme in the 1990s, undertaken to stop them from being used as hideouts by Shi'i guerrillas opposed to his regime. Many dams and canals ordered to be built by the dictator have now been

Hind also had many fond memories of holidays in Iraq. 'It was January in Kurdistan,' Hind told me. 'We were perched on our mules, which moved slowly along the edge of the ravine, deep in contemplative thought. One of the adult riders looked tenuously down the gorge, wondering where he would end if the sure-footed mule slipped. The youngsters in the group looked longingly across the panorama of white mountains, pines, gorges and deep ravines, wanting to tumble, to throw snowballs, or simply to roll in the snow. We were heading to Shaqlawa to spend our holidays in this land of magic and snow, having never seen or touched snow in Baghdad.'

❦

In 1957, Margaret's contract at the university changed from that of a foreigner to that of an Iraqi employee, as she was married to and naturalised as an Iraqi and had become a Muslim.

The family left the al-Alwiya district and, for a short time, rented a house in the well-to-do district of Mansour in west Baghdad. Mohamed was building a house for the family in Mansour: it was a striking blend of international style and purely local and traditional motifs, and featured an ingenious round library. 'That house had a wonderful intimacy,' in Kanan's description. 'It had no overall structure. It just grew organically as our circumstances permitted, its morphology at one with nature in the form of our garden – wall, brick, sheet glass – and at any moment you could hardly tell if you were inside or outside.'[3] In another interview he recalled: 'On the main wall of our Mansour house a Ben Nicholson painting was turned into a huge relief mural, echoing a theme also carved into the front door. I recall my father scratching about with a stick on some wet stucco in that house when I was ten years old. The harshness of the newly poured surface was irritating to him; he needed to break

---

demolished, allowing waters from the Tigris and Euphrates rivers to flood back and the fish and fowl to return.

Mohamed Makiya and Gropius (Pic: Bob Mottar, Life Magazine 2.1.67)

it up, to relieve the natural oppressiveness of the material.[14]

Hind also had fond memories of the Mansour house, with its brick ceiling built by *Ustad* Hassan. 'It had a very long corridor, which ended at the library of antique books Mum and Dad collected. It was a wonderful length to throw a ball for our dog, Casca, who went running and finally crashing into the books because of the marble floor. The corridor was the area we escaped to during one of Iraq's coups d'état, to hide from the bullets we heard in the garden and which came into the sitting room and ricocheted out on the other side.' The Makiya home in Mansour was the envy of many people in Baghdad: it was both modern and traditional. The family lived in the house for thirteen years, until 1971.

※

The late fifties until the early seventies were the most enjoyable and prosperous years in Baghdad for the Makiyas. During the late 1950s, famous architects converged on the city when King Faisal's government embarked on a series of architectural commissions, most of them modernist in spirit. The Italian Gio Ponti designed a building for the Ministry of Development and the Development Board; the Greek architect Constantinos Doxiadis designed massive housing schemes to accommodate the migrants who were flowing into Baghdad; the German Walter Gropius submitted plans for Baghdad University; and the Swiss-French Le Corbusier designed a new stadium and sports complex, later the Saddam Hussein Gymnasium. Frank Lloyd Wright, pre-eminent American architect of the time, designed a cultural centre for Baghdad, incorporating an opera house, a university, museums, shops, restaurants and a zoo.

Mohamed entertained Gropius, Wright, Gio Ponti and the Spaniard Josep Luís Sert in the Mansour house. 'When Walter Gropius came to my house in Baghdad,' Mohamed told Guy Mannes-Abbott, 'I criticized his design for the University of Baghdad campus, built in the '50s, because [. . .] to me, it had no character or intimacy, nor the closeness that even Cambridge had. Most of my colleagues don't believe in tradition. To me the modern really has to have an identity and a philosophy. And the philosophy is the trinity of human values – man, space, and time. These are three. They become the human scale.'[5]

Through thick and thin, Margaret was Mohamed's backbone – the unseen creator of the man. Without her he would never have become the architect that he emerged, as Margaret organised receptions for his colleagues and for famous international architects; she was the mediator between her husband and the outside world.

☙❧

It was the heyday of East-West cooperation and exchange, championed by the Development Board created by Iraq's strongman and fourteen-times Prime Minister, Nuri al-Said. The Board's first six-year plan (1951–56) focused on infrastructure: flood control and irrigation projects to help develop agriculture. The next plan (1955–60) centred on investment in transport and public buildings. The Board also made improvements in the run-down areas of Baghdad, but they were minor compared with those implemented in the Qasim years.

Beginning with the 1956–57 budget, money was set aside for the Iraqi Museum, the royal palace, new Parliament buildings, law courts, sports complexes, a national library and an opera house. Each spring the next round of major projects would be announced with pomp and ceremony, while the ones completed that year were dedicated by the King with equivalent formality.

Mohamed, always mindful of the city's history, was eager to take part in the modernisation of Baghdad: this was the abiding passion of his life. The city was witnessing its most prosperous period in 700 years. The King envisaged a new style of urban architecture that paid overt tribute to the ancient cultural traditions of Mesopotamia, and Mohamed was determined to ensure that Iraq's cultural heritage was respected and represented in new constructions. He tried to influence the Development Board, the institution appointed to lead the country into the modern era, which had most of Iraq's oil revenues at its disposal. As one of the young architects supposedly educating the Board, he was frustrated and disappointed that he was only able to take part in some informal discussions. He suggested alternatives to the practice of commissioning British architects.

When Mohamed looked at the architectural heritage that had been left by the region's ancestors, he felt that the current generation had a duty to maintain this legacy and develop it for the sake of future ages. He believed that the architect should go back to the architectural tradition of the region to get some insight into its techniques and to the spiritual and aesthetic values that informed it, and draw on these to create a new architectural civilisation.

That Mohamed was not comfortable with modernism in and of itself became increasingly clear as he submitted proposals for the development of Baghdad. He was convinced that modernism was a healthy reaction to what had gone before. But for him there was something missing: the identity of the region of which Iraq was a part. As he once proclaimed in a lecture, 'I'm for preserving the local character with modernism, rather than imposing modernism as an international language of appreciation.'

CHAPTER 6

The Iraqi Artists' Society

*'I was a stranger [to Iraqi artists in the fifties] because I am
not a painter, and they thought that painting alone was art.
I believed in applied art, and they looked down upon it.
To me, the carpenter and the blacksmith are artists.'*

Mohamed Makiya's journey through the world of architecture began during his university days and continued throughout his life. Another journey, which also started when he was at university, was a journey through the world of art.

Mohamed's artistic journey started from what could be called 'dead sources', as suggested by his son, Kanan, in his book on Mohamed's architecture, *Post-Islamic Classicism*. The 'dead sources' for Iraqi art represent the cultural heritage of Islamic times and that of Mesopotamia (Assyria, Babylon and Sumer).

Mohamed was fond of portraying architecture as the mother of all arts. He described the relationship between architecture and art as like that between a tree and its branches: one could not exist without the other, as architecture is an art form. Arabesque (a complicated decorative design, made with many lines that curve and cross each other) and calligraphy are, according to Mohamed, examples of both fine and functional art which are natural extensions to the elements of a building's architecture.

Iraqi art started to blossom during the 1950s, in work that reflected the country's identity and invoked Babylonian and Sumerian themes. This was especially evident in the work of Jewad Salim (1919–61), the father of modern sculpture in Iraq, and his Baghdadi school, of which Mahmoud Sabri (1927–2012) and Faiq Hassan (1914–92) were members. They called for the establishment of an Iraqi Artists' Society – a first for the country. It was fortunate that Iraqi statesmen and businessmen as well as the royal family were interested in the arts; the British Embassy also promoted art and regularly organised exhibitions for British artists. Iraqis who had studied art in Britain, Italy and other European countries, including Jewad Salim and Atta Sabri (1913–87), exhibited at the embassy's cultural centre.

When he was studying at Cambridge University, Mohamed also attended lectures on art and literature and acquired a good knowledge of art. When he returned to Iraq he was eager to bring together Iraq's artists, and to provide a platform that would cultivate Iraq's artistic identity. His unique approach to architecture involved incorporating art into a building's design – and this led to a life-long friendship and partnership with Jewad Salim and his British wife, Lorna.

On 7 November 1955 the lawyer Khalid al-Jadir invited several artists to his house and proposed the setting up of an association for artists. He was an amateur artist himself, and his legal expertise came in handy in drafting a memorandum of association. The first meeting was attended by Iraq's leading artists – Jewad Salim, Yousef Abdul Qadir, Nouri al-Rawi, Ismail al-Shaikhli, Mahmoud Sabri, Naziha Selim and Khalid al-Qassab, among others – along with the architects Mohamed Makiya, Rifat Chadirji and Qahtan Madfai. The artists continued meeting in 1956, along with a number of architects and other professional people interested in the arts. Makiya was elected as the first president of the Iraqi Artists' Society.

In his memoirs, Khalid al-Qassab, who was a heart surgeon as well as an amateur artist, recalled that Makiya was chosen as president even though he did not get the most votes: Faiq Hassan got the highest number and Jewad Salim the second highest, but Salim insisted that Makiya be the head of the society. The other artists agreed, because Makiya was good at public relations and had excellent connections with the government and with intellectuals in Iraqi society.

Makiya took on the responsibility of registering the society with the Ministry of Interior on 11 January 1956, and persuaded the government to give it a plot of land in the Mansour area.* Ahmed Naji al-Said described how 'Mohamed envisaged a school of Iraqi art inspired by traditional art, but many of the artists of the 50s favoured modern art. Salim designed a logo for the society based on a statue of Gudea, the Sumerian king, which is still in use. The secretary was the famous poet Bulland al-Haideri. Margaret was friendly with the British politician Desmond Stewart, a man of letters, as well as with John Haylock and Alan Lane, all [of whom] taught English literature at Baghdad University, and these family friendships helped to develop the society.'

In an interview with me, Al-Said described the society's important events. 'The first event [of the Society] was the Iraqi Art Festival in the spring of 1956. In his opening speech, Makiya stated that art is more than paintings and sculpture, and that the Society would also promote archaeology, architecture and local crafts in addition to holding exhibitions and showcasing the work of Iraqi artists.' The festival became one of the main events in the cultural calender of Iraq, supported by prominent writers, musicians and journalists, as well as by the political hierarchy.

The festival included an exhibition, at the al-Mansour Club, of Jami'yat al-Ruwad (the Pioneers Group), founded in 1950 by Faiq Hassan, the father of modern painting in Iraq. Among its members were Jewad Salim, Khalid al-Qassab, Yousef Abdul Qadir and Mahmoud Sabri. The work of the Pioneers was avant-garde, depicting local scenes and landscapes in Iraq with aspects of Impressionist and post-Impressionist styles.

The al-Mansour Club was chosen as an exhibition venue because Mohamed was friendly with the president of the club, Ali Haider al-Rikaby, whose father had been Prime Minister under Faisal I. Ri-

---

* In 1962 the Society constructed its own building, designed by Qahtan Madfai, which is still being used today as its headquarters.

Jewad Salim in conversation with King Faisal II (3rd from left) in the company of Mohamed Makiya. The artist Mohamed Sabri appears on the right side of the photo next to Jewad Salim. (Pic: Makiya Archive)

kaby also happened to be Makiya's neighbour, and their sons went to the same school.

Although successful, the exhibition at the al-Mansour Club was limited by the size of the venue; some of the artists who could not show their work set up their own competing exhibition, which attracted the attention of the media.

To ensure that this did not happen again, a much larger venue, the Olympic Club, was chosen for the next exhibition. On Makiya's instructions one of the artists, Mahmoud Sabri, got in touch with the palace, and Makiya met with King Faisal II, whom he found very engaging and humble. The King, who was a keen painter and a student of Sabri, was offered an honorary membership in the Society and inaugurated the exhibition on 10 May 1957. In line with Makiya's philosophy it was an inclusive event, with 200 paintings, twenty sculptures and thirty architectural models, as well as furniture designs, ceramics and photography. There was also a selection of architectural drawings by Mr and Mrs Madloum, Rifat Chadirji and Qahtan Madfai, as well as by Mohamed Makiya himself.

Frank Lloyd Wright – architect, interior designer, writer and educator, who had designed more than 1,000 structures, 532 of which were completed – was one of the guests of honour. Wright was visibly impressed by Jewad Selim's *Pastorale*, a plaster relief (of a rural scene from southern Iraq) in which Selim made an artistic breakthrough by lifting the figures off the surface of the flat plaster behind them and placing them on different planes, thus greatly enhancing the three-dimensionality of the finished result. Makiya had a brief but intense professional relationship with Wright, who was in Iraq in the late fifties at the invitation of King Faisal, to assist in designing buildings that it was hoped would rejuvenate Baghdad. Makiya later recalled that Wright was rather arrogant.

When approaching mid-twentieth-century Baghdad, both Makiya and Wright returned to tradition as a basis for their architecture and identified their historical sources as key elements in articulating the cultural identity of the city. Wright admired and was inspired by the Abbasid dynasty and the ancient Assyrian and Sumerian civilisations, while Makiya drew his inspiration from the Abbasid, Seljuk and Safavid cultures. Wright referred to 'what genuinely belongs to the Iraqi people' while Makiya was more interested in the aura he believed surrounded ancient ruins. They both opposed the intrusion of Western concepts of materialism and commercialism and their impact on the Middle East.

༄༅

Mohamed got the idea for an annual New Year's party for the Iraqi Artists' Society from his time in Britain, and from the New Year's celebrations he had attended in the Chelsea Town Hall in London's King's Road during his student days in London. The Iraqis welcomed the festivities, and even the King was invited. He was not able to attend, but sent the Prime Minister and a number of ministers. Foreign diplomats working in Baghdad also attended.

The Society organised lectures and invited famous personalities as speakers, such as the Egyptian art historian Zaki Muhammad Hassan, well known for his book on Fatimid art; he spoke about the contribution that Islamic art could make to modern art. There were also talks by architects such as Rifat Chadirji, a famous contemporary of Mohamed, and Kahtan Awni, an Iraqi architect educated in Europe who took part in projects commissioned by the Iraqi Development Board.

Distinguished visitors to the Society's activities included the author Agatha Christie; she accompanied her second husband, the archaeologist Sir Max Mallowan, to Iraq. The trip inspired her novel *They Came to Baghdad*. Christie was very disappointed when a work by Faiq Hassan she wanted to buy had already been sold. The Doxiadis firm bought expensive works by Jewad Salim, and the British Council bought a collection of Iraqi paintings; Mohamed himself bought *Pastorale*, the plaster relief that so impressed Frank Lloyd Wright. At that time the Iraqi upper and middle classes had not yet developed a taste for contemporary art, so the main buyers were the British and other foreigners. Many Americans also bought Salim's works.

The Iraqi Artists' Society also organised other important exhibitions, such as a major display of the works of Kadhim Haider, a member of the Pioneers Group whose work focused on the figure of the urban labourer. The exhibition included forty paintings collectively known as 'The Matrydom of Hussein'. Another exhibition, by the artist and sculptor Muhammad Ghani Hikmat, took place in Mohamed's Mansour house, as there was nowhere else to hold it. Muhammad Ghani would later create some of Baghdad's highest-profile sculptures and monuments.

Baghdad had changed almost beyond recognition in the first half of the twentieth century. Summarising some of the most visible developments, Gerald de Gaury, a British army officer and Arabist and a close friend of the Iraqi royal family, noted how paddle steamers, camels, horses and horse cabs had given way to public buses, taxis, private cars, bicycles and a tramway. Once dependent on word of mouth and a solitary government newspaper, Baghdad's contact with the outside world was now mediated by fifty Iraqi and regional Arabic newspapers, along with radio stations, television channels, and a number of European publications. Where only recently education had been limited and restricted to *madrasas* (colleges of Islamic theology), in which religious lessons were conducted in Arabic, students could now improve their prospects at secondary, technical and law schools and could learn a foreign language, usually English.

As de Gaury reported in *Three Kings in Baghdad: The Tragedy of Iraq's Monarchy*: 'Many women had abandoned the strict, age-old conventions surrounding their sex and were "largely emancipated". Oriental singing and dancing, including boys impersonating women in theatres, had shifted towards more Europeanised cabarets, and cinemas showed Western thrillers and surprisingly risqué films with no shortage of flesh on display. Alcohol was freely available, especially at the nightclubs that sprang up in the more affluent neighbourhoods. Glass-fronted shops, crammed with the latest luxuries such as televisions, fridges and washing machines, lined the streets, where the occasional Rolls-Royce slummed it with oversized Cadillacs, Buicks, Chevrolets, Fords, Oldsmobiles and the doughty Vauxhall Veloxes. Sartorial codes had changed too. The traditional Arab dress of flowing robes and headdress now competed with close-fitting European suits, shirts and ties. Although the popular diet of rice, unleavened bread, kebabs, dates, milk and arak liquor remained largely intact, the way of consuming it had evolved. Fewer ate with their fingers and [they] had turned instead to knives, forks and spoons.'[1]

De Gaury went on to say how life was 'less glamorous and considerably more deadly' for the majority of Iraqis. Baghdad's population had swelled, but infant mortality was high in the overcrowded slum areas. Poorer people sweltered in summer and shivered in winter. To an epidemic of eye diseases were added typhoid, tuberculosis, cholera and malaria.

The years leading up to the monarchy's overthrow were turbulent times in Iraq. The golden days of the monarchy came to an end with the nationalist coup led by Abd al-Karim Qasim in 1958. (In 1959, a young Saddam Hussein fled from the street after an assassination attempt on Qasim, in which he had participated.) The royal family was brutally killed, and Frank Lloyd Wright certainly did not endear himself to the new regime by describing his projects as 'worthy of a king'. The first and second Baathist coups would follow, in 1963 and 1968.

But Mohamed's life centred on his work as an architect, and for him, there was only architecture. 'My father is an architect in every fibre and pore of his being,' Kanan wrote in *Post-Islamic Classicism*. 'I marvel at how he remained one for forty years in the teeth of the social upheavals and political turmoil of Iraq, quite apart from the normal passage of time which does so much to temper the youthful idealism in us all. Most other professional men and women of his generation got sucked into the whirlwind's vortex, and spewed out. Not him. Events seem to have passed him by, like routine weather reports.'[2]

As the sectarian violence which followed the ousting of Saddam Hussein in 2003 was reducing Baghdad to rubble, Wright's grandiose schemes were being reappraised, and respect for Makiya's philosophy of combining traditional and modern styles in a happy symbiosis was gaining acceptance as a possible way forward for the troubled capital.

꙳

The 1958 nationalist revolution was a watershed in Iraq's modern history. Fortunately it did not see the end of cooperation with foreign architects. Mohamed and Margaret had a close relationship with Constantinos Apostolou Doxiadis, a Greek architect and town planner who became known as the lead architect of Islamabad. Doxiadis worked in Baghdad between 1959 and 1962 and produced a master plan for the city of 3 million inhabitants, retaining the historic souk. He did not try to reproduce Baghdad's patterns for the newly planned residential districts; instead, he broke down the traditional residential areas into a polycentric network of 'neighbourhood units' or sectors modelled on the post-war British new town, favouring pedestrian movement. He was also commissioned to produce a model housing plan for what is known today as Sadr City, a huge sprawl of slums that housed Shi'i migrants who came to work in Baghdad.

Mohamed and Doxiadis became friends, and he and Margaret were invited to discussions that Doxiadis organised for prominent people to contemplate issues like housing and education. Makiya spoke at these meetings and was part of the circle of friends and associates who got to know Doxiadis when he was working in Baghdad.

The foreign architects worked very hard and took their projects extremely seriously. Despite their efforts, however, in the end only three of the five major projects commissioned by the Iraqi Development Board were built: Walter Gropius's Baghdad University, for which the contract was awarded in 1959; Gio Ponti's Development Board headquarters building; and Le Corbusier's Gymnasium, finally completed in 1980, long after the architect's death in 1965. (The Gymnasium was, along with the works of foreign architects generally in Baghdad, the subject of a seminar presented during the Baghdad Capital of Culture celebrations in 2013.)

After the King was killed in 1958, Mohamed lost no time in promoting the Iraqi Artists' Society to the officers who had staged the revolution. On 21 July, a week after the revolution, he wrote a letter as president of the Iraqi Artists' Society to the new leaders of Iraq, emphasising the role of art and architecture in expressing the values of freedom and liberation. The aim of the letter was to get permission for the Society to continue its activities, to make it clear that the artists were on the side of the people, and to reassure the officers who carried out the coup that the fine arts community was not elitist:

> The letter Makiya wrote to [Qasim] was very important, as the best artists in the country were affiliated in one way or another with the royal family,' Ahmed Naji al-Said explained in interview. 'All of these artists had scholarships that were sponsored by the royal family. When the revolution happened, what Makiya was trying to do through that letter was to send a message to [Abd al-Karim Qasim] to say that [. . .] maybe the artists were associated with the royal family, but they are actually revolutionary, and all the topics they depict in their artworks deal with the poor and the hungry and the masses that your revolution is trying to represent. Instead of excluding these artists [. . .] you should actually use them in your revolution to create a new visual language for your revolution.

And that is what happened: it was a masterpiece of diplomacy. Perhaps Mohamed's greatest trait was his ability to find some common ground that could be the basis for defining a common interest on the part of parties with different interests.

Just as he had ingratiated himself with the monarch, Mohamed found favour with Abd al-Karim Qasim. He discussed his ideas for the conservation of date palm groves and the building of housing complexes in the shadow of the date palms with his friend, the contractor Umran Tawfik. Tawfik knew Abd al-Karim Qasim during his army days and acquainted him with Makiya's views. Qasim met with Makiya after the revolution, and following the meeting issued a law prohibiting the cutting down of date palms and the building of roads through date palms. He also talked of streets lined with date palms and of a square in Baghdad with palms, but the idea died when Qasim was killed in the 1963 Baathist coup.

While he was in power, Qasim supported artists and sponsored a number of group exhibitions. The government commissioned Jewad Salim to design the famous Nasb al-Hurriyah (Freedom Monument) of 1958.

The meaning and impact of the monument are described by Kanan Makiya (using the pseudonym Samir al-Khalil) in his 1991 book *The Monument: Art, Vulgarity and Responsibility in Iraq*:

> It is a visual narrative of the 1958 revolution, told through symbols which the artist had been developing in the whole body of his work. Strikingly modern, yet clearly paying homage to its sources in Assyrian and Babylonian wall-relief traditions, the monument is organised as fourteen separate bronze castings averaging eight metres in height. These are meant to be 'read' like a verse of Arabic poetry, from right to left, from the events leading up to the revolution, to the revolution itself and an ensuing harmony.[3]

Rifat Chadirji was selected to develop the site for the monument, as well as for other monuments, including his own Unknown Soldier Monument and the Freedom Mural by Faiq Hassan. All this public art was for the first time being commissioned from Iraqi artists. When certain religious elements in Iraqi society wanted to demolish the Freedom Monument, which they considered un-Islamic as it depicted human forms, Mohamed waged a successful campaign to ensure its preservation.

꧁꧂

In 1965 Makiya opened the first art gallery in Baghdad. He called it the al-Wasiti Gallery as a tribute to Yahya al-Wasiti, whose twelfth-century drawings were remarkable examples of Baghdadi visual art that documented the architecture, costumes, colours and events of Abbasid Iraq. The gallery ensured the continuity of a long tradition that was being modernised with avant-garde art. In 1968, Makiya coauthored a book called *Baghdad* with three leading historians: Mustafa Jawad, Ahmed Sousa and Naji Marouf. It has a separate section on al-Wasiti and the Baghdadi painting tradition.

Reflecting on his involvement with the arts, Makiya observed to Guy Mannes-Abbott:

> I was a stranger to [Iraqi artists in the fifties] because I am not a painter, and they thought that painting alone was art. I believed in applied art, and they looked down upon it. To me the carpenter and the blacksmith are artists. . . the other artists think art must involve a canvas. Canvas in a climate like ours! It's odd. So I said, we paint on the wall! We use ceramics, we don't use brushes. Jewad Salim always supported me because he's very intelligent. The others were very obsessed by ideas about painting. I never painted in my life![4]

Makiya emphasised that, influenced by his experience of the Chelsea Town Hall Arts Festival, he wanted to create an arena for all the various disciplines and groups of artists, including the Baghdadi group and the Naïve and Impressionist schools. He wanted to secure government recognition of the Iraqi Artists' Society. When talking to London friends about the Society he said, 'I tasted brief success but bitterly regret the twists of fate that were to decimate the hopes of this liberal-minded generation of thinkers – a generation who had begun to question the rigidity and narrow nature of Arabism, a generation of socialist intellectuals who could have taken Iraq into a very different future for itself and the region.'

In addition to promoting the works of Iraqi artists, Makiya built up his own large and important collection of around 150 Iraqi artworks by the country's most renowned artists, including Jewad Salim, Shakir Hassan al-Said, Faiq Hassan, and Muhammad Ghani Hikmat. A complete set of the work of David Roberts (1796–1864), a nineteenth-century Scottish artist who was commissioned to draw the route from Cairo to the Holy Land, was also in his collection.

Salim's art featured prominently in Makiya's collection. He obtained in the early 1970s a number of Salim's sketches. Both Makiya and Salim wanted to establish continuity with the past while remaining modern.

Salim once made a sketch that was used as decoration on silver boxes traditionally made by Sabean silversmiths in a technique dating back centuries. Mohamed Makiya's granddaughter Bushra received this box as a special gift, which included the following note from him:

> I would very much like for you to have this silver box, which I commissioned in Baghdad sometime in 1959 or 1960. It was made in the traditional way Sabean silversmiths used and practised for centuries in Iraq. Their techniques [were] a secret known only to themselves, and they have, sadly, disappeared in modern times. I collaborated on this project with Jewad Salim, who provided the sketch you see inscribed into the metal. This was an early example of the kind of collaboration Jewad and I pioneered between the fine arts and traditional craftsmanship. Jewad and I were trying to give these crafts a new reason to exist in the modern world, and I went on to collaborate with craftsmen in architectural projects like the Khulafa Mosque and many others.

The editor of the book *The Makiya Collection of Modern Arab Art*, Diddi Malek, emphasised that meeting Jewad Salim was a turning point in Makiya's life. 'Makiya never thought he would one day collect the letters and sketches of his artist friend, but that is what he did, in addition to some of Salim's important drawing and sculptures.'[5]

In another book she edited, *The Dr Mohamed Makiya and Kufa Collection of Works by Jewad Salim*, Malik says: 'For Mohamed Makiya, Salim's way of thinking in visual art is the essential complement to his own architecture; they both understood that a fundamental correlation existed between them, between art and architecture, and sought to realise it in practice while always respecting each other's space. Salim clearly valued the view of Makiya in relation to tradition and modernising Islamic architecture; and at the same time Makiya emphasised that his architecture required precisely the new visual vocabulary and symbolism that Salim was so brilliantly developing, in his arabesque forms and ever so distinctive crescents and domes.[16]

Makiya requested artists to create three-dimensional sculptures when a monument or mural was required for a public institution. The successful marriage between architecture and art that Makiya referred to as applied art was most evident in the work of the sculptor Muhammad Ghani Hikmat, one of Salim's students. Makiya was instrumental in getting Muhammad Ghani to use the abstract form of Arabic letters and Arabesque motifs as the basis for his sculpture, and commissioned him to carve a wooden door for his own house in the al-Mansour district of Baghdad while it was still in its early design stages. In 1969, he commissioned Muhammad Ghani to design a door inspired by Kufic script for the new Rafidain Bank in Kufa.

Makiya was concerned that many Iraqi artists had become Westernised, and were inspired only by European art. He noted that Henry Moore was interested in Sumerian art, while some Iraqi artists were preoccupied with Michelangelo. One of Makiya's objectives was to bring artists' salon conversations to the public – to flesh out ideas through discussions before a wider audience at forums organised by the Iraqi Artists' Society. For him, lectures and seminars set up by the Society were as important to the promotion of Iraqi art as were exhibitions.

The purchase of artworks, artefacts, antiques and curios was Makiya's passion throughout his life. He always stayed in touch with artists, organised exhibitions for them, and socialised with them.

CHAPTER 7

The Khulafa Mosque

'I had to build a cathedral in an area suitable for a chapel. I tried to design the mosque as it might have been in Abbasid times and to make a mural that carries scenes and Arabic calligraphy which shows the history of the mosque and echoes the history of the minaret.'

At the end of the 1950s, Mohamed Makiya's architectural practice was growing from strength to strength. Mohamed's first important commission – one that would eventually bring him international acclaim and establish his reputation as an architect who could integrate a contemporary building into its historical setting – was the Khulafa Mosque project. It was initiated in 1960 by the Ministry of Religious Affairs (Awqaf), which wanted a mosque designed around the dilapidated ninth-century al-Ghazl Minaret.

Kanan told me that the Khulafa Mosque was the first paid commission his father received as an architect. 'Previously he had been designing people's houses, for which he did not get any money. Sometimes he got a carpet. Once [as we have heard] he got a cow! Then came a real commission for a real building – incorporating a ninth-century minaret. This was perfect for my father.'

The mosque would be located not far from the Makiya family home in the Sabbabigh al-Aal neighbourhood, in the centre of Baghdad, an area of the city that Mohamed loved. It was initially named after textile workers who used to work there and were known for dyeing garments with black and crimson red, representing the martyrdom of Imam Hussein and his family in the seventh century. The original name of the neighbourhood was al-Ma'munia, referring to the Abbasid caliph al-Ma'mun (786–833 CE), who resided in a large complex that included a private mosque for the Caliph, referred to as the Caliph's Mosque or, in Arabic, *Jami' al-Khalifa*.

The original Khulafa Mosque (again known as the Caliph's Mosque, and also the Palace Mosque, *Jami' al-Qaṣr*), was built, with its minaret, in 902–908 CE; the minaret fell down in 1271 CE and was rebuilt in 1279 CE. The Caliph's Mosque was the focal point of religious activity during the last four centuries of Abbasid rule (958–1258 CE). Prayers were said at the mosque for eminent figures who had died. Religious debates were also held there.

The later Suq al-Ghazl (spinning souk) Mosque was built by Suleiman Pasha in 1193 AH/1779 CE on the western part of the same site. The Suq al-Ghazl Mosque (but not the minaret) was deliberately demolished in 1958, either by the Municipality of Baghdad (*Amanet al-'Aṣima*) or by the Board of Development (*Majlis al-I'mar*), and most of its site was incorporated in the extension of the new Queen Aliya Street, renamed Jamhuriya Street after the abolition of the monarchy on 14 July 1958; it was renamed yet again as Khulafa Street after the building of the new Khulafa Mosque. Makiya was asked by the Ministry of Awqaf to design it in detail, and to supervise its construction to completion in 1960–65.

The commission was to restore the minaret to its former glory and afford it a mosque that properly complemented it. Makiya tried to design the mosque as it might have been in Abbasid times; he wanted to make a mural that carried scenes and Arabic calligraphy showing the history of the mosque and echoing the history of the minaret.

He was concerned that bricks were being taken from the site of the minaret, and wrote to the Baghdad Municipality asking them to stop selling pieces of land that surrounded the minaret. He also insisted that new buildings should not be higher than the minaret.

In his book *Post-Islamic Classicism*, Mohamed's son, Kanan Makiya, devotes an entire chapter to the Khulafa Mosque. Kanan studied visual design and architecture at the Massachusetts Institute of Technology and studied regional and urban planning at LSE. When he was fourteen, he accompanied his father around the construction site of the Khulafa Mosque. (In 1975, Kanan became Managing Director of the London Branch of Makiya Associates.)

In an interview, Kanan described how Mohamed battled with the Ministry for two years. 'He worked relentlessly on coming up with ideas for the project, none of which he showed the client for a very long time. He was constantly bombarding the client with letters of how important this project was. His intention was to try and get the Ministry of Awqaf to give him a plot of land worthy of the minaret. This went on and on with increasingly testy and irritated letters backwards and forwards until finally my father was threatened by the Ministry with having the whole project taken away from him. He responded by quickly turning out a design – the one that was built.

'But his conflicts with the Ministry of Awqaf did not end there, because soon they were complaining about other things. When the dome went up, the Ministry said that my father had put a Christian cross all over the outer dome as the covering design of the dome. The brickwork on the dome was very nicely done by the last remaining generation of craftsmen builders. So there was a huge conflict, with letters to the newspapers backwards and forwards – Are these crosses or are these not crosses? – and my father was able to show that this pattern had historical roots. The Ministry of Awqaf had simply misread it as a Christian cross.'

⊱⊰

As the site was too small for the conventional positioning of a large dome on a rectangular building, a concrete dome in correct proportion to the minaret was built as a separate entity. The pair of *riwaqs* (arches) are set apart from the dome and one of them doubles as an entrance gateway. The focal point of the Khulafa Mosque project was the restoration of the Suq al-Ghazl minaret. When the project

The Khulafa Mosque

Khulafa Mosque (Mohamed Makiya Archive, courtesy of Aga Khan Documentation Center, MIT Libraries – AKDC@MIT)

was completed, it emerged as a structure with three distinct parts: the minaret, the mosque with its dome and prayer hall, and the enveloping *riwaqs*.

According to the architect Dr Subhi al-Azzawi (invited by Mohamed in the 1960s to be a member of the Cultural Committee of the Kufa Gallery), 'The design of the Khulafa mosque is that of an "unfinished business", of a "work in progress", of a "working out" of principles, of architectural and building elements, of structural systems, and of constructional techniques and detailing, as well as of Islamic integral geometric decorations and Arabic calligraphy.' It is 'a very clever assembly of architectural spatial volumes and of building elements brought together to signify the meaning and spirit of what a true mosque should incorporate. The whole ensemble is a setting to show off the minaret in all its architectural visual glory, historically and presently as well as aesthetically.'

Makiya loved and respected Iraq's traditional master builders (*Ustawat Mi'mariyoun*) and relied upon them extensively in the construction of the Khulafa Mosque. The master builders did not have offices; they met their clients in Baghdad's coffee- and tea-houses. And that is where Mohamed did business with them in the traditional Arab style. He would tell these skilled artisans about the houses he was designing, and they would go to build them, with loving care and attention. A symbiotic relationship developed between Makiya Associates and Baghdad's master builders and craftsmen, nourished by the personal affection that had grown between them and the architect.

Yet officials from the Ministry of Awqaf were not happy with Makiya's work and did not invite him to the opening of the mosque. Instead, the Ministry wanted to put him on trial for designing a mural with crosses, which they regarded as Christian crusader symbols, seemingly unaware that crosses were part of typical Abbasid decoration. The ministry also challenged the accuracy of the *mihrab* (a niche in the wall of the mosque indicating the direction of Mecca), though a survey showed it was more in line with Mecca than that of any other mosque in Baghdad.

※

Until 2006, the Khulafa Mosque was well preserved. Today the ninth-century minaret is leaning perilously and is in danger of falling. The Makiya Foundation Consultancy Forum for Baghdad, an organisation established by Makiya's students, is writing reports and urgently lobbying to try to ensure its preservation.

'All the government's funds and resources have been devoted to the war against ISIS, and the municipality is virtually bankrupt. It has not got money to spend on Baghdad,' Kanan observed. 'Intellectuals are trying to raise funds from outside and are putting pressure on the government to preserve the mosque before there is a catastrophe. There has been no maintenance for at least ten years, but the mosque is fixable. It is a shadow of its former self simply because it has not been taken care of.'

※

When he completed the Khulafa Mosque in 1965, it was inevitable that Makiya would be labelled an 'Islamic architect'. But as Kanan points out in *Post-Islamic Classicism*: 'The Islamic faith did not impose a physical setting or set of visual symbols by which to identify it. The first Muslims took pride in worshipping wherever they happened to be, and their faith developed very "purely", lacking both a clergy and any corporate notion of identity and hierarchy.'[1]

Kanan also comments that 'Makiya may or may not be an Islamic architect. At bottom this is a matter of opinion, or definition. None the less he is unquestionably the first Iraqi, and probably the first Arab, architect to have tried to reappropriate a specific, hitherto "dead" monumental tradition of built form associated with Islam. This is a more meaningful prism through which to consider his contribution to architecture.'[2]

The Khulafa Mosque design and its implementation was an Iraqi architectural journey which Makiya continued throughout the rest of his life, as the design philosophy behind it influenced all his subsequent work and projects.

CHAPTER 8

The School of Architecture

> *'The architecture school [at Baghdad University] drastically changed the training of Iraqi architects and had a tremendous impact on how Iraqi architecture would be defined. Like experiments that were also taking place in the visual arts and literature under Makiya and other instructors, the school sought to establish a modern Iraqi architecture that had roots in the country's history and traditions. Stimulated by the vibrant cultural and political scene around them, they were inspired by different paradigms of Iraqi history.'*

When Mohamed Makiya returned to Iraq in 1946, there was no school of architecture at Baghdad University, which was teaching only civil engineering and did not regard architecture as a discipline worthy of its own department. There was no school of architecture in the Middle East. He met the dean of the engineering college, was given a frosty reception, and was advised to work in the engineering college and forget about architecture.

Architecture was viewed as a bastard form of engineering in which real science was mixed up with the 'fine arts' in a hodge podge that made no sense to an engineering mindset. From Mohamed's point of view, engineering was a wholly secondary discipline, below architecture and entirely subordinate to it. This was a view that stayed with him his entire life. Architecture was, in his mind, the most humanistic of disciplines.

And so, in spite of the social pressures to abandon his profession, Mohamed volunteered to give free lectures on architecture to civil engineering students. 'If they do not agree to a separate department, at least they could add architecture within the engineering department as a subject in the final year. I tried to achieve this temporarily, until the opportunity came to establish a separate school for architecture. I managed to convince the engineering college to add two hours a week for the study of architecture for final-year students – but it was considered an additional subject, for which the students did not have to pass an exam, as they were just studying it out of interest.'[1]

When talking to his friends in London about returning to Iraq Mohamed observed that living and studying for eleven years in Britain had turned him into a stranger to those who were stuck in their old ways. For them, architecture was limited to building aesthetics: it was considered a narrow, superficial specialisation. For him, architecture was an interesting social, philosophical, economic, educational and moral discipline, which meant the architect must have a comprehensive, all-encompassing background. He had more respect for the 'traditional', oral, coffee-house culture than he did for the intellectual milieu around him. For Makiya 'traditional' education was not found in books – his uncle was very intelligent and, though he didn't go to school and couldn't read or write, he knew so much that Makiya remained in awe of him. Makiya believed knowledge is acquired through dialogue and discussion and is encouraged by the built environment.

It was in search of this sort of knowledge, as a student in Liverpool, that he took his bicycle and toured the British countryside. The pub was the nearest thing he could find to the Arab coffee-house, and he spent many an hour in various hostelries, from the Lake District to Devon. He felt that it was necessary, as well as enjoyable, to meet working people and develop an appreciation of their changing environments. His dedicated study of the northern environment and climate enabled him to put his own life into perspective. To work through and with people rather than impose alien ideas on them became his creed. He believed that knowledge of local traditions and environments should be drawn on as a background for any new development, material or otherwise.

Makiya described a professional architect as a trustee – like an archbishop. 'He is not a salesman or a builder, or a developer who must work to please the client. Architecture is not a craft, it is an art.'[2]

At the beginning of 1959, thirteen years after Mohamed first suggested the establishment of a school of architecture, he was invited by the dean of the College of Engineering to start one. A committee of three architects (himself, Midhat Ali Madloum and Qahtan al-Madfai) was formed. In 1959 he was able, with the assistance of his two colleagues, to set up the school, as part of the engineering department. The school's curriculum included courses in planning, architectural design and interior design, supported by extensive courses in architectural history (including Islamic architecture), building technology and architectural representation.*

After the decision had been made to establish the School of Architecture, Mohamed suggested creating sub-departments to broaden the curriculum so as to include the arts and social sciences. Among the subjects introduced were photographic imaging, geography, sociology, ceramics, documentation and Arabic calligraphy. This was not an easy task, because the school's lecturers and those in authority did not welcome change. The school started with a small number of lecturers, mostly part-timers. They were paid according to the number of lectures they delivered.

Many of the school's lecturers came from Eastern Europe. There were the Czech architect Jan Čejka and the Polish artist and educator Zofia Artymowska. A number of Eastern Europeans taught at the school and also worked on the new master plan of Baghdad designed by the Polish State Planning Office *Miastoprojekt-Kraków* and administered by the Central Agency for Foreign Trade, Polser-

---

* Midhat Ali Madloum and Kahtan al-Madfai were well-known architects of the 1950s who were responsible for the construction of high-rise buildings in Baghdad.

vice. Makiya was always eager to recruit professors from overseas, but his attempts were not always appreciated, as that meant taking work away from Iraqis.

'Makiya shopped for good professors, good tutors,' according to Ali Mousawi, one of his students who studied at the school from 1964 to '65. 'He was good at finding architects, creating them, and looking after them. He brought Polish, Czech, American and British teachers here – all different nationalities. He picked the right ones. Professor George was a top professor in the history of architecture. He would say: "I don't want my students to memorise how many windows a building has. I want them to understand why they are studying the history of architecture. I want them to see why this building is good and beautiful."

'Makiya was always trying to upgrade the standard of teaching in the school. Unfortunately it has deteriorated now.' In Mousawi's view, 'The problem is that the new architects are very much affected by this new movement of post-modernism and deconstruction.'

Makiya was pushing his students in the direction of creating a new style for the Arab world by combining the motifs of his beloved Islamic tradition with the achievements and new materials of modernist architecture. He lectured extensively about Islamic art and Baghdadi painting, with a focus on the work of Yahya al-Wasiti, whose manuscripts from the twelfth century documented life in Abbasid Iraq.

The students were constantly made aware of their own environment and country and urged to look beyond its borders to the immediate region. Makiya wanted them to do measured work or field work in the city they came from. Before that, he had them undertake a study of the house they had grown up in: the kitchen, the bedroom, the living room. This was usually the first architectural assignment they were given in the school.

'He wanted everyone to be aware of his identity, but at the same time to look at it as one piece in a very large mosaic,' Ahmed Naji al-Said observed. 'He had the ability to look at history in global abstract terms and at the same time to look at individual components and their uniqueness and see how they contributed to a larger picture.'

Makiya's vision of teaching architecture depended heavily on other arts and social sciences being taught alongside architectural core subjects. He engaged Lorna Salim, wife of Iraq's master sculptor Jewad Salim, to teach landscape painting, the landscapes in question being purely Iraqi. Muhammad Ghani Hikmat taught sculpture and Faraj Aboo taught fine art.

Influenced by his measured work in the Cotswolds, Makiya also wanted his students to preserve the fading architecture of Baghdad. He and Lorna Salim took the students with them on a field trip to explore Baghdad, and to produce sketches and photographs for architectural measured works. Dr Jala Makhzoumi was one of Makiya's most accomplished students. One of her measured work drawings along the banks of the Tigris was done under Salim's supervision.

Makiya's London students recall being asked to use the spring holiday to conduct an architectural survey of their own town and neighbourhoods through photos and drawings. He encouraged them to go to the local councils to ask for plans and surveys. The aim of the project was to assemble a collection of photographs in order to create a comprehensive archive on Iraqi cities that would become the nucleus of an architecture library. Makiya wanted to enlarge the understanding of 'the civil engineer's view' of the architect and to incorporate architecture within different specialisations.

There was a lot of emphasis on practical work and design. Students had to present their designs to a committee of lecturers who criticised their work and gave advice. In the final year, when the students presented their theses, specialists were called in to evaluate their work. If a student designed a medical complex, the staff of the medical college would be called on to give their opinions.

There was also an important emphasis on Iraqi heritage, and students took field trips outside Baghdad to study the traditional houses of the southern marshlands regions; the guesthouses of

Baghdad, Karbala and Najaf; and the public baths and traditional houses in Baghdad and other Iraqi cities. Some projects focused on door-knockers and other items.

One of the important projects of the school involved making drawings of the riverside of the Tigris in Baghdad. Small boats were the best means of transport and gave the students the opportunity to survey the banks of the river, as they moved slowly, and from a distance suitable for taking photographs. Makiya divided the students into groups, with each group responsible for a certain section of the riverfront. These photos were then transferred into drawings.

Subhi al-Azzawi, coming from a family of Iraqi master builders (*Ustawat Mi'mariyoun*) spread over three generations, recalled how much Makiya admired his taking modern scientific instruments to Baghdad in May 1971. Sourced from the Bartlett School of Architecture and Planning (University College, London), they were obtained in order to measure the microclimatic conditions and internal thermal environments of indigenous courtyard houses over a period of twenty months, as part of al-Azzawi's PhD field work research. He discovered that ideal ventilation was achieved through the use of traditional architectural design concepts and principles. Al-Azzawi recalled that, being an environmental designer, Makiya very much welcomed his findings, which simply confirmed his beliefs about the advantageous characteristics of traditional courtyard houses.

But it was not only the buildings on the banks of the Tigris that students measured, photographed and drew. In the early 1960s, when Makiya was the Head of the School of Architecture at Baghdad University, he established a programme for his students to survey, measure and individually draw traditional Iraqi courtyard houses in Baghdad and Kadhimiya, along with a whole street in the Sinak neighbourhood of Baghdad. These drawings were still kept in the same department when al-Azzawi last saw them in 1971–72.

In all these endeavours, Makiya put his whole being at the disposal of his students, who loved and respected him. He was always eager to hear about their adventures and achievements when they had something to do with architecture. For Ali Mousawi, Makiya was a lot more than a tutor. 'He was like a father to me,' he explained. 'He told me that he had wanted his son Kanan to be an architect, but he did not do that, so he wanted me to follow in his footsteps instead.' Many people spoke of their relationship to Makiya in a similar fashion – and for his part, Makiya had a reciprocal feeling toward his students: they were his family.

Ali Mousawi recalled that Makiya always encouraged him to regard himself as an architect. 'Don't ever think of yourself as a draughtsman,' Makiya told Mousawi. 'Don't follow anybody. Be yourself.' Makiya gave Mousawi the courage to proceed in the way he wanted to proceed – to follow his heart – and all the time he was monitoring his student's activities to see how he was doing. Makiya also encouraged Mousawi to record and protect the history of Baghdad, and he sent him to take measurements of two bathhouses that were 1,000 years old. Those drawings were in the Baghdad University's archives until they were stolen from the university after the 2003 American invasion.

Attared Sarraf was another of Makiya's early intake of students, joining the School of Architecture when it was set up in 1959 and completing the five-year degree course. 'Makiya set up the school assisted by those around him, but he was the driving force,' she told me – 'without him it would not have happened. He had a lot of energy. He was very enthusiastic; the school was his baby. He treated it more like a project and acted more like a project manager than a head of school. The tutors taught in the morning and went to their architectural offices to work in the afternoon. Many of the students wanted to stay late in the school and continue their studio work, as they did not have proper drawing boards at home. But the rules of the university did not allow this. Some worked in architectural practices in the evening. It was a new development for students to work as well as to study at a university.

'Once, to celebrate Eid, a group of about eighty were taken to Hatra by Dr Makiya. We stayed in the huts used by archaeologists.

Makiya with his students, including Akram Ogaily (President of the Makiya Foundation) 1963 (Pic: Akram Ogaily)

It was the greatest time of our lives when we were students. We were all Iraqis – it did not matter if you were an Arab, a Kurd, a Sunni or a Shi'i. There was a great belief that we would be working for the whole country. My friends who are living in Iraq today say we were very lucky to be students at that time.'

Like Ali Mousawi, many of Makiya's students – including Akram Ogaily, who later worked with him on the Kuwait State Mosque project – emphasised that he wasn't a typical lecturer, who just delivered his lectures and marked assignments. 'His lectures were combined with interesting anecdotes and stories,' Ogaily recalled. 'He was rather like a father who directed his students to appreciate the responsibility of architects, as architecture required a response to social and environmental needs.'

Ogaily has a vivid memory of his first meeting with Makiya. 'It was in 1962. He asked me why I wanted to study architecture, and when I told him because I want to serve my country, he replied that I could join the army if I want to serve my country. Architects have to be devoted to their profession.' Ogaily studied at the School of Architecture from 1963 to 1967 and was first in his class every year. He also recalled Makiya shouting at a student who suggested that a historical area in Baghdad should be replaced with a new development. 'Dr Makiya called him a criminal and said he should not be studying architecture.

'Dr Makiya organised social events and parties and invited students to his place. Once when the dean of the College of Engineering refused to let the students at the School of Architecture hold a party in the college hall, Dr Makiya took the thirty-five students to his house!'

Maysoon Wahbi was an architecture student when Makiya was Head of the School of Architecture. She was not taught by him, but she has fond memories of invitations to his house in al-Mansour. In her view, 'It was a very modern house, with the best architectural library in Iraq.'

Wahbi also remembers what she described as 'the nice small library' in the School of Architecture at Baghdad University, which had architectural journals, magazines from overseas, architectural records and reference books. 'Dr Makiya was strict. He wanted quality. He had a soft character, but he was tough at the same time. There was no place for politics in the school. He was a real academic, concentrating on academic affairs, architecture, and art – not politics. He kept his students focused and was always there for them. Anybody could go and see him.'

Makiya had rigid criteria for admission to the School of Architecture. 'The head of the school is limited by the criteria of the average marks of the competing applicants,' he recalled when speaking to Rashid al-Kahoun. 'This is what happened with the now-world famous architect [the late] Zaha Hadid,* who was a candidate for the school and whose application contained recommendations from two friends of mine, Kasim Hassan and Ahmed Sousa. I was under pressure to admit her from her father, Muhammad Hadid, who was Minister of Finance after 1958 and a leading figure in the National Democratic Party. Despite my sympathy for her – I knew how eager she was to be an architect – her average marks were less than those of other candidates. I waited for one of the other candidates to withdraw so she could be allowed in according to the rules, but this did not happen.'[3]

When he interviewed prospective students, Makiya used to present them with the problems and difficulties of architecture, and through questions and answers he could judge whether the candidate was suitable to be an architect. He emphasised that architecture was not like writing a book or drawing a picture that can be revised or changed.

Makiya appreciated students who adopted a critical approach to architecture and questioned their professors. Ogaily remembered an assignment given by Professor Abdallah Ihsan Kamel, who asked the students to design a statue of al-Kindi (a Muslim Arab philosopher, polymath, mathematician, physician and musician). 'The assignment was not clear, and one student named Sabah pointed this out and explained that that was why he did not produce a design. Professor Kamel was very angry with him, but Dr Makiya agreed with the student's argument and said that such an attitude should be adopted by good architects.'

In an article about the history of the School of Architecture one

---

* Zaha Hadid was an Iraqi-born British architect, the first Arab woman to receive the Pritzker Architecture Prize and the first woman to be awarded the Royal Institute of British Architects Gold Medal. She created highly expressive, sweeping, fluid forms of multiple-perspective points and fragmented geometry that evoke the chaos and flux of modern life. Her acclaimed work includes the Aquatic Centre for the London 2012 Olympics, the Board Art Museum in the US and the Guangzhou Opera House in China.

of its current professors, Ghada al-Silq, noted that under Makiya's leadership between 1959 and 1968 it addressed major social issues, such as the acute housing shortage caused by rural-urban migration and the destruction of traditional buildings in Baghdad.

※

At the end of the 1960s, Makiya was frustrated that, owing to barriers of red tape and academic resentment, his dream of establishing an independent department of architecture would never be realised at Baghdad University. Meanwhile, Makiya Associates was expanding its work to the Gulf States. In 1965 the Bahrain Chamber of Commerce held a competition for the design of its building and Makiya Associates won. New projects were on the horizon, and in 1968 Makiya decided to resign as Head of the School of Architecture.

Makiya reconciled himself to the fact that a stage in his life had come to an end. As someone with 'new' ideas, he was seen as a threat to the status quo and had to be content to find salvation in an inadequate educational system. Such intransigence afforded, and continued to afford, him a great deal of heartache and regret.

But Makiya never fully let go of his students, and the lecturers and students in the School of Architecture never forgot him. In 2006, at the age of ninety-two, he returned to a hero's welcome as a celebrity – a visit organised by his son, Kanan, and Mustafa al-Kazimy, then Director of the Iraq Memory Foundation founded by Kanan in Baghdad and a staunch friend to the Makiyas. Mohamed discovered that a lecture hall had been named after him. When the students complained that they did not have enough books, he became very upset and told them they did not have to wait for books or for a teacher: he urged them to use technology, Google, the internet to find the information they needed. 'Everyone was surprised,' al-Kazimy recalled when talking to me. 'A man of ninety-two talking about technology and the internet and telling them to find information themselves.'

The School of Architecture

Makiya visiting the Department of Architecture at Baghdad University, 2005 (Pic: Makiya archive)

Collage showing Mohamed Makiya at the top of a pyramid looking down on students at the School of Architecture since its establishment in 1959 (family archive).

Makiya's meeting with the students lasted for hours and kept Makiya away from other commitments. It was a very emotional time for him: he felt he was back in the 1950s. 'His eyes were filling with tears,' remembered Dr Ghada al-Sliq, who had helped to organise the meeting. 'It was very moving. He did not stay in the office for even a few minutes; he wanted to talk to the students right away. All the students were very eager to see the legendary Dr Makiya – they had often heard about him. He told them to ask him questions, and they asked him about the establishment of the school and how it was in the 1960s, and about his own vision of architecture in Iraq and its future. So he started to talk about what he wanted the young generation to do in Baghdad, especially in the old areas. He asked them to go back to their Sumerian identity, to feel the brick and the mud and to see the cities, with their open areas and green areas. "I will back you all the way," he said, "and if I have more years to come, I will give you all that I have: pictures, knowledge."'

When the students in the School of Architecture at Baghdad University heard that Makiya was in hospital, shortly before his death, they produced a remarkable collage in the form of a pyramid with Makiya's image on top and photographs of the graduates of the school from every year since its foundation under the watchful eye of their mentor.

Khalid al-Sultani, the renowned architect and a former lecturer in the school, said: 'When we, the lecturers, students, and former graduates of the school, organised a celebration in 1984 to commemorate the twenty-fifth anniversary of the school, we were filled with satisfaction and pride to see the results of the blessed and healthy seeds that were planted by its founder, Mohamed Makiya. It is now a huge tree, blossoming with the fruits of intelligent students and experienced graduates who enriched the built environment of their country and the neighbouring countries with their distinguished designs.'

The School of Architecture still adheres to Makiya's philosophy, and he is very much alive in the hearts of his students. The section of the website of Baghdad University dealing with the College of

Engineering, of which the School of Architecture is a part, echoes his views: 'Inspiration should come from the architectural heritage of the Arab world in general, and especially from Iraq and its historical roots.'

Kufa University

Makiya also wanted to establish a private, non-governmental university in Iraq. He chose the town of Kufa for this university, which he hoped would regenerate the south of the country. His scheme was very ambitious. Makiya Associates, the architectural practice he established in 1946, prepared detailed plans for a university town. An educational brochure about the proposed Kufa University stated that the objective was to create a university that would serve 20,000 students.

Makiya envisaged that an agricultural college, with sufficient land to produce agricultural products, would be attached to the university. The Sea of Najaf would irrigate the land, whose produce would be sold in a specially designed marketplace. Colleges for art and literature and religious studies – as well as, of course, architecture – were also planned.

The idea for the university came to Makiya after he visited Kufa in the early 1960s. He enlisted the support of a number of Iraqi academics and Shi'i businessmen, extending to the passive support of the Shi'i religious establishment. The idea was discussed in detail with Dr Kadhim Shubar, a highly regarded medical surgeon, the scholar and lawyer Mahmoud al-Mudafar, and the prominent businessman Hussein Shakri, who were all very impressed with it. Donations from prominent Iraqi businessmen, and gifts of land in the Kufa region, flowed in to the Founding Committee Makiya set up in Baghdad. Makiya had a way of becoming passionate about a project in a way that was infectious.

But from the moment they came to power in 1968, the incoming new Baath regime saw the ambitious project as sectarian, and they used the excuse that it was envisaged as a private university to shut it down, claiming that the society set up to administer it did not have enough funds to build a university. In truth, the Baathists refused to acknowledge the place of, or need for, any independent institutions of learning.

To add insult to injury, a new Baath development minister came up with a kitsch money-making scheme and ordered Mohamed to design a hideous resort on the site of ancient Babylon. Mohamed says he told him, "'This is crazy. You are asking me to turn Babylon into a tourist trap with a Ziggurat hotel. This is a crime against history!" The man was my worst enemy at the time – he was the one who had ordered Kufa shut down – but he listened, and I managed to convince him. Later they [the Baathists] killed him.'[4]

The Baath regime at the end of the sixties and early seventies was brutal. When Mohamed was on a business trip in Bahrain in 1971, Margaret learned that his name was on a newly created blacklist, on account of alleged connections with the Freemasons (see next chapter.) She advised her husband not to return to Iraq and followed him into exile the following year, in 1972.

Even though the Kufa University project ended abruptly in Iraq, Makiya never stopped dreaming about it; he kept the plans and drawings, and often talked about it. When he first proposed the idea of a new university in Kufa there were only four universities in Iraq: two in Baghdad, one in Mosul and one in Basra. By the end of the 1990s every province in Iraq had a university; there was a government university in Kufa, but nothing like the one Mohamed had proposed. After settling in London Mohamed opened the Kufa Gallery, a Middle Eastern cultural centre showcasing contemporary Arab art. He called the London gallery 'Kufa' because he saw it as a continuation of the project in Iraq that never materialised.

During a celebration of the life of Makiya in London organised by the Iraqi Academic Association in 2011, the then-Iraqi cultural attaché Dr Abdul Razzaq Abdul Jaleel al-Issa, the former chancellor of the Kufa University established by the government, was invited to give a speech. He showed slides of the government-designed Kufa

University, which Makiya criticised. He told Dr Abdul Rahim Hassan, who sat next to him during the presentation, 'This is rubbish.' Makiya gave al-Issa a copy of the designs for the university he had proposed in the 1960s, and he kept the dream alive until he died.

CHAPTER 9

Leaving Baghdad

'I was like Isabel Burton [wife of the legendary British explorer]. Pay, pack and follow – that was her motto, and it became mine.'

Until 1971, Iraq was good to the Makiyas. In addition to the Khulafa Mosque (1963), there were many other lucrative commissions: the Rafidain Bank in Kufa (1968), the Rafidain Bank in Karbala (1968), the Mosul Museum (1968), and the College of Jurisprudence in Baghdad (1968). Makiya also designed educational buildings for Baghdad University, as well as the College of Theology, the Ministry of Foreign Affairs, the Ministry of Municipalities in Baghdad, the Directorate of the Baghdad Water Board, and numerous residences, along with the public library in Karbala. Margaret was a respected teacher at Baghdad University.

In 2002 Margaret told her granddaughter Bushra about her experiences as a teacher of British history at the College of Arts and Sciences in Baghdad University. Bushra related their conversation in a paper, 'Teaching in a Foreign Country,' submitted for a writing course at the Massachusetts Institute of Technology (MIT) in the late 1990s.

Margaret recalled that grading was her least favourite part of teaching, and moving to Baghdad certainly didn't change that. In addition, the teaching methods and curriculum were taken straight from the British system and were no different from what Margaret had been used to in England. Because the university wanted its students to become more fluent she taught almost entirely in English, although she began to incorporate phrases of Arabic as she became more comfortable with the language. This meant she had to speak clearly and couldn't take anything for granted. However, the real difference between teaching in Britain and in Iraq was the driving need for good marks, and perhaps a willingness to indulge in dubious devices to obtain them at exam time.

'My grandmother emphasised that many aspects of British influence, at least within the university, were accepted without question during her first few years in Iraq. No one ever doubted the quality or relevance of the curriculum, which she described as "not designed to meet the needs of the new country",' Bushra wrote.

British influence was perceived strongly in many ministries, where the British Embassy was even referred to as *Abu-Sami*, meaning 'father of the exalted' in Arabic. All events, good or bad, were often ascribed to this sinister influence.

Margaret recalled that she learned more from her students than they did from her, and that getting an insight into another culture was the most important thing she gained during her years in Baghdad. Iraqi culture and society infiltrated daily life in the university. For her the greatest privilege was not to be able to think as other people think, because that was impossible, but merely to be privileged to understand some of the complexities of others' lives.

Margaret had to adapt her teaching style to this different way of thinking and to the different concerns of her students who, unlike their British counterparts, were struggling to find their place in an ever-changing society. For instance, when she taught sociology at a women's college for a year, she decided to organise a series of visits to different places rather than simply teach a theory-based class. She took her students to prisons, hospitals, courts of justice and even an experimental farm, and said that the experience was just as much an eye-opener for her as it was for them.

Most women in her classes led secluded lives based on home and family and therefore did not have much exposure to this realm, although there were women doctors with impressive post-doctoral degrees from European medical schools.

However, only an extremely limited number of women had access to higher education. In 1958, 21 per cent of Iraqi girls (compared to 62 per cent of boys) attended school at the primary level. The number in higher education must have been only a small fraction of this. Compared with 20,154 elementary and secondary school teachers, there were only approximately 600 university teachers in the country.

This meant that classes were very small, consisting of only nine to fifteen students. Classes rapidly rose to fifty or sixty, as college education became free after 1958 and literacy rates rose. But, even in such a small room, there was a lot of self-segregation, and it took a very daring woman to talk with men during breaks. While male-female relations definitely relaxed during Margaret's time in Baghdad, women were never completely free.

'However, the hope, eagerness and enthusiasm that her students brought to the classroom crossed these gender boundaries,' wrote Bushra. 'All my grandmother's students were hopeful and highly engaged, no matter what their social class. While some were driven to college by drivers every day, others lived in mud huts, known as *sarifas*, on the outskirts of Baghdad. Yet every one of them was motivated by the hope of finding something better, even if it was simply a minor government job. Hope for change, freedom and intellectual curiosity were driving elements in college society.'

Margaret told her: 'The happiest moment in teaching is when a student asks you a question and makes you think, and you realise that you can't answer that question satisfactorily to yourself or to the student.' These moments, more than anything else, are why she looked back on teaching in Baghdad as one of the happiest and most fulfilling times of her life.

Margaret's years in Baghdad coincided with years of major political upheaval in Iraq, and politics soon came to dominate life within the university. With the emerging middle class and technical developments that had grown during the 1930s and 40s, people became more and more dissatisfied with the traditional outlook. This discontent, combined with the exploding student population – any student who passed the secondary school exams could enroll in college, and the population of Baghdad doubled between 1922 and 1947 – made it harder and harder to maintain academic standards. Student demonstrations came to interrupt academic life more and more frequently.

☙❧

By the end of 1956, when unrest was growing, Margaret took a break from the turmoil of Baghdad and went to England for her mother's funeral. With sadness in his voice, Kanan speaks about never having met his mother's family, even though he and Margaret took regular summer holidays in England; Margaret's family continued to shun her for having married an Arab. (Margaret had a brother who was also in conflict with his father and was also disowned, partly because of his drinking problem; Margaret gave him money to keep him going.) After the funeral Margaret returned to Baghdad, where the unrest continued, and in 1958 a secret organisation within the military led the revolution that overthrew the Iraqi monarchy.

After the revolution, students were becoming more involved in politics and less in academic pursuits, and the university became a more oppressive and political place. Government suppression was so strong and powerful that it infiltrated the organs of life and state. There were no protests or demonstrations except for the official ones sponsored by the government, which students were required to attend.

'One day, the then-president of Iraq, Abd al-Salam Arif, visited the university for the day and observed my lessons,' Margaret told Bushra. 'While he probably didn't understand very much because he didn't speak English . . . you could have heard a pin drop in that room.' Arif had replaced Abd al-Karim Qasim, who had become President after the 1958 revolution but soon clashed with extremist elements and lost popularity because of his erratic behaviour and inability to manage the clash of pan-Arab nationalists and socialist

The Makiyas at the Acropolis (family archive)

forces. Qasim was ousted in an extremely violent coup in 1963 and executed the next day. The coup was carried out by the Arab Baath Socialist Party, with the assistance of the army.

After the Baathists had seized power in 1963, Ahmad Hassan al-Bakr became Prime Minister and Abd al-Salam Arif President. The Revolutionary Command Council was put in charge of policy-making. But divisions within the party resulted in a lack of clarity and cohesion. After nine months of this regime, in November 1963 military officers mounted a bloodless coup. Abd al-Salam Arif was invested with much greater power, remaining President until 1966, when he died in a helicopter crash, to be replaced by his brother, Major General Abdul Rahman Arif.

The Kurdish insurgency continued to undermine the government's authority, while Arif's hands were to a large extent tied by the military men who had put his family in nominal charge. When attempts were made to give the Kurds a greater degree of autonomy, the army chiefs voiced their disapproval. However, not even the army was united. Two high-ranking supporters of Arif, Colonel Abd al-Razzaq al-Nayef and Ibrahim al-Daoud, staged a successful coup but were unable to cement their position since they lacked popular support. The well-organised Baathists had little trouble in overcoming the newcomers, and were back in government in 1968. They had learned from their previous mistakes and clung to power until 2003.

※

Although both Mohamed and Margaret worked hard, they always made time for adventure. In 1962, Mohamed decided to take one of several car trips from Baghdad to Europe and even to Moscow, which was behind the Iron Curtain at that time. He drove his car, which had an Arabic number-plate, into Red Square. His niece Amal has fond memories of the trip: 'We went through Syria, as there was trouble in Beirut, and then through Turkey. Kanan and Hind were with us, and Margaret was reading the maps.'

The trips took around three weeks, with the family accompanied by Lilly Joseph, the nanny. They passed quickly through Turkey and visited various European capitals. Mohamed once fell asleep at the wheel after a large meal of Turkish kebabs; Kanan grabbed his hand on a twisting mountain road in Turkey, and he woke up and slammed on the brakes. Two of the car's wheels were over the edge of the cliff. A passing lorry driver pulled the vehicle back onto the road, and the journey continued.

Hind remembered eating the best ice cream in the world in Damascus. It was pistachio flavoured. 'Our journey back to Baghdad was memorable, too. I learned something about my father's driving, and his daydreaming. To him, the window of the car was a large piece of paper, on which he visualised designs. He was always distracted by the next project. We once drove through a desert road, with a large inlaid Damascus chest, with its mirror, on the car's roof. We passed some Roman ruins. From the back of the car, I remember saying: "Dad, I do not remember seeing these ruins before. Where are we now? What country?" I remember a lengthy lecture on my poor observation of all that is visual around me. He was a tough father, but I always felt I could wrap him around my little finger. I was, after all, his little girl.'

In Venice, Mohamed and Margaret organised their journey so that they would pass through the city at the time of the famous art festival, the Venice Biennale. The children would be parked in a café nearby, to quietly read comic books, while Mohamed and Margaret went off on their cultural jaunts.

☙❧

Both children, Kanan and Hind, went abroad to study, and were not in Iraq when disaster struck and their parents were forced into exile after an arrest warrant was issued for Mohamed: Kanan was in the United States and Hind in the UK. After completing his A levels,* Kanan was accepted by King's College in Cambridge, but he would have had to wait for a year because he was too young. One of the Jesuit fathers at Baghdad College convinced his parents to send him to MIT, to his mother's eternal regret. He left Iraq in 1967 and, apart from a summer break in 1968, did not return until 2003. Hind went to the University of Bristol, where she studied architecture.

The coming to power of the Baathists instigated a bloody reign of terror. At the beginning of 1969 a public spectacle was made of the hanging of nine Jews accused without evidence of spying. Saddam Hussein was rising rapidly within the Baath Party and during the 1970s worked tirelessly to consolidate his power base.

A narrow, family-based elite continued to hold the reins of power in Iraq, despite attempts by the Baath Party to institutionalise its rule. By 1977 all of the most powerful men in the Baath Party were related

---

* The A Level (Advanced Level) is a subject-based qualification conferred as part of the General Certificate of Education, as well as a school-leaving qualification offered by the eductional bodies in the United Kingdom to students completing secondary or pre-university education.

to either Saddam Hussein, Ahmed Hassan al Bakr or General Adnan Khairallah Talfah, Hussein's brother-in-law. They held key positions in the the party, in its ruling Revolutionary Command Council and the cabinet, and all were members of the same family from Tikrit.

When in 1973 a planned coup organised by the Security Chief, Nazim Kazzar, failed Kazzar was executed. The Baath Party and the Iraqi Communist Party combined to form a National Front. Socialist rhetoric did not prevent the private sector from trebling during the 1970s, and by 1980 most of the hundreds of multi-millionaires in Iraq had connections to the Baath Party. The capitalist tendency did not extend to a pro-Western foreign policy. Relations with the West were poor, while those with the Soviet Union warmed and the Soviets kept Iraq supplied with weapons.

On 16 July 1979 President Bakr was ousted and Saddam Hussein assumed the power he had always craved. Not only was he now President of the Republic, he was Secretary General of the Baath Party Regional Command, Chairman of the Revolutionary Command Council and Commander-in-Chief of the armed forces. Iraq was now re-created in his image, ruled with an iron fist and controlled by an all-seeing, all-knowing security apparatus that had a grip on every aspect of life within the country.

The security forces had a list of subversives, and Makiya's name was on the list. He was accused of being a member of a sinister conspiracy of Freemasons. In the fifties a British colonel had served as a military adviser to the Iraqi monarchy. A meticulous man, he had kept records that showed that he was a Freemason. He fled when the army overthrew the monarchy in 1958, leaving his files behind. Twelve years later the Baathists found them. Makiya's name was among those of numerous guests the colonel had invited to his many parties. The Baathists suspected a vast conspiracy of Freemasons and British imperialists, and secret policemen were therefore preparing to arrest everyone named in the files.

One of Margaret's ex-pupils alerted her to the crisis. It was clear that her husband was in danger of his life, though fortunately he was out of the country, working on a project in Bahrain. Margaret was able to warn him to remain there while she used her connections to relocate the family away from Iraq.

The Makiyas' beloved house in the Karadat Maryam district, where the family lived before they were forced into exile, was requisitioned by Adnan Khairallah, Saddam Hussein's brother-in-law and cousin. Margaret said she hoped whoever took the house would be cursed. In 1989, Khairallah died in a helicopter crash that was officially labelled an accident, but his disputes with Saddam suggested that he was assassinated on the dictator's orders. The story of the house in Karadat Maryam had a happy ending, though. During the 2003 war, it was occupied by twelve American lieutenant colonels. Kanan insisted on seeing it and was given permission to use it as the headquarters for the Iraq Memory Foundation, a non-governmental organistion (NGO) which he established.

For Margaret, 1971 was a dreadful year. She made a superhuman effort to get the family's extensive book and art collection out of Baghdad: 'I was like Isabel Burton [wife of the legendary British explorer Richard Burton],' she recalled. '"Pay, pack, and follow" – that was her motto, and it became mine.' As unobtrusively as possible, she worked to pack her family's belongings and ship them out of the country. Every object, every book, had to be inventoried; every form required a separate protocol of signatures. 'I was lucky,' she says. 'I'd been teaching twenty-seven years by that point – twenty-seven times, say, a hundred students a year. That made for a lot of contacts in the various ministries, and I had to draw on every single one of them.'[1]

❦

Mohamed's and Margaret's library embraced the culture of the Middle East and the wider Islamic world, as well as its connections with Europe. It also represented the particular interest of Margaret in accounts of European travellers (especially women) in the Middle East, and of Mohamed in Islamic art and architecture. The library was therefore rich in books on art and design, archaeology, travel, history, literature and, of course, architecture. The impressive number of volumes mentioned in the Sotheby's catalogue prepared for the library's sale in London in 2016 attested to the tremendous appetite that the Makiyas had for collecting books. From the early 1940s, they were indefatigable buyers of any second-hand or antiquarian volumes that touched on their interests – from recent scholarly studies to rare colour-plated books and literature on the Middle East – as well as of collections of old photographs, postcards, drawings, watercolours, prints and maps. The 300 books offered at Sotheby's attracted strong bidding, soaring more than six times over the pre-sale estimate.

Commenting on Makiya's love of books, Yasmine Allawi, one of his former employees, recalled that 'One of the books he had was enormous. He said he bought it at an auction for £6,000 in the eighties. That was the cost of a flat at that time. He said, "Open this one – look at it." When I opened it, it had hand drawings in gold. [They were of] Napoleon's invasion of Egypt. It was amazing. I asked him what he was going to do with all these books, and he said it was his wish that they be placed in a library in Najaf. He wanted a library that would contain all these books.'

Zina Allawi, one of Hind's classmates, remembered visiting Margaret shortly before she left Iraq, never to return.[2] 'She was there on her own in the house. Dr Makiya was not there, and the children had left. She was packing to leave for Bahrain. She is one person who is really very solid, very cooperative, very supportive, very rational. She does not jump to conclusions – very orderly, the exact opposite of Dr Makiya. Dr Makiya was passionate and all over the place, but she was always there behind him. She was a very, very nice lady. When you are young you always have somebody that you look up to, and Auntie Margaret was a person I looked up to. I always called her "Auntie Margaret". Her students absolutely adored her.'

---

* Zina Allawi and Jihan Winter referred to Margaret as 'auntie' as a sign of affection and respect, even though they were not related to her.

Jihan Winter (née Allawi) commented that, while she liked all her mother's friends, Auntie Margaret was her favourite. 'I remember that she used to teach Hind and I sewing and crafts when I visited and made encouraging noises when we showed her the masterpieces we had created.'

Margaret joined her husband in Bahrain in 1972. Her pension from Baghdad University was one of the most important things she lost on account of the move. A new chapter, living and working in exile in the Gulf and then in London, began for the Makiyas.

For Mohamed it was a time of progress, hard work and achievement. But for Margaret, the happiest years of her life – her life in Baghdad – were over, and she started suffering from cyclical bouts of depression, which never left her.

CHAPTER 10

Makiya Associates and Architecture in Exile

*'Traditional continuity should not mean living in the past.
It should be a question of the past living in the present
for a better future.'*

Although one door closed for Makiya in Iraq with his forced exile, many new doors opened in the form of lucrative contracts in the Gulf states: Bahrain, the UAE, Kuwait, Oman and eventually Saudi Arabia. In the Gulf, he soon became one of the most sought-after architects and designed a number of important new mosques, including the Kuwait State Mosque (1984) and the Sultan Qaboos Grand Mosque (1993). A significant number of projects were awarded through competition. He also submitted working drawings for the Arab League headquarters in Tunis. In addition to mosques, Makiya Associates designed cultural and community centres; art galleries, cinemas, libraries and a racecourse; shops and supermarkets; diwans, hotels and car parks; residences and guesthouses; rental and low-cost housing units; city gates; government buildings; and universities. The firm also undertook restoration of traditional houses.

The commissions were varied and challenging. In Bahrain, they included the Isa Town Gateway (1973), the al-Baharna Residence (1972), a Centre for the Handicapped (1977), the Sheikh Mubarak Building (1977), the al-Baharna Hotel (1976), and the Bahrain National Oil Company headquarters (1976). Makiya Associates also designed the Ministry of Finance and the Wattiyah Housing

Complex (both in 1975). Markets included the wholesale market in Dubai (1983); the al-Hitmi market (1981) in Doha; the meat, fish and poultry market in Qatar (1983); and the Diera Retail Market in Dubai (also in 1983). One of the last commissions in the Gulf States was the Sultan Qaboos Grand Mosque in 1993, when Quad Design was appointed as lead consultants, with Dr Makiya as the chief design adviser.[1]

The first Makiya Associates office established in the Gulf was the Bahrain office, which had been opened before, in 1967. In 1968, Makiya's firm won an international competition to design the Chamber of Commerce and Industry in Bahrain. Bahrain was the first port of call for Mohamed after exile from Iraq in 1971. Professor David Oates, head of the School of Archaeology in Baghdad, had succeeded in arranging a fellowship for Makiya at the University of Cambridge, but Mohamed chose to focus on projects in the Gulf rather than on academic pursuits.

Makiya Associates, as it was now known, became an international consultancy, with a head office in Bahrain and eventually a service office in London to support the head office. Branch offices followed in Muscat, Kuwait, the UAE and Qatar; the office in Qatar took charge of the supervision and implementation on site of specific projects.

An introductory brochure describing the internal organisation of Makiya Associates stated that the head office handled design and project management, with a particular emphasis on site survey, implementation, client liaison and supervision of projects in various countries. The head office was also the financial and administrative centre of Makiya Associates and the place where Mohamed spent most of his time. It was organised into three departments: design, project management and general administration. The office in Bahrain was staffed with architects and engineers, including a resident engineer as well as supervisory and administrative staff.

As Kanan Makiya noted in *Post-Islamic Classicism*: 'Local traditions in Bahrain, in addition to those in Muscat, left an impression on many of [my father's] buildings of the 1970s. In fact he fervently believes that a Bahraini building must read as if it could only belong to Bahrain. Is a poet not obliged to know the language in which he writes? Similarly an architect (whatever his nationality) who has not studied long and hard the nuances of expression in Bahraini architecture has no right to "butcher" traditions – as he would put it – which have taken centuries to evolve.'[2]

Makiya was critical of foreign layouts imported to the Middle East, as in the case of a European design that was used in a low-cost mass-housing complex in Bahrain. The residents of the complex did not like the design, and Makiya went to the site and, in traditional Arab style, drank a cup of tea with some of the people who were housed there while listening to their needs.

When thinking about designs for the Gulf States, Makiya sought to define those elements and qualities of the traditional buildings of the Middle East that were relevant to the design problems he faced. In Manama, Bahrain, Makiya obtained a lease on an empty site and built an office and housing complex. It was a single-storey bungalow style of construction, and the Makiya family as well as the architects lived in and worked from the complex all though the 1970s and early 1980s. Makiya's designs in Bahrain were highly regarded: the Isa Town Gateway, built in 1973, was put on Bahraini stamps, book covers and in guidebooks, and Mohamed's reputation as an architect grew correspondingly. The Gateway was built on a shoestring budget, reflecting Makiya's contention that his architecture did not always require large amounts of money.

'The aim of the project,' states the Aga Khan Trust for Culture, 'was to create a civic monument in the form of a gateway for the recently constructed Isa Town development. The design of the gateway is inspired by gateways of the Arab-Islamic tradition. The gateway is composed of five arched galleries; two identical lateral ones for pedestrian circulation, and two larger central ones for vehicular circulation, the latter connected by a higher, but narrower central arcade. The abstraction of the traditionally vaulted gate is expressed by a series of parallel arched fins which through their rhythmic repetition create the volumes of the gateway.'[3]

But even though Makiya Associates was one of the most respected and successful architectural practices in the Arab world, there were three major problems that dogged the firm. Makiya may have been a creative genius, but he had no administrative skills. He could not break away from the Arab tradition of involving his family in his business, giving them managerial positions for which they were not qualified. Kanan admits that when he graduated from MIT, where he studied visual design and architecture, he was too young and inexperienced to become a managing director of the London office. Makiya's brother's son Nazar, who had no architectural qualifications, was similarly put in charge of the Bahrain office.

The second problem was Makiya's occasionally incendiary temper. When someone incurred his wrath he would humiliate and abuse them – without, it seems, being aware that he was doing so. In 1971, Yousuf Dawood was the primary architect working on the house of a Bahraini minister, Jawad al'Urayidh. Makiya was not in Bahrain during the crucial period when the design of the house was approved, and when he saw what Dawood had produced he flew into a rage, as he did not like the building's rigid grid. The rooms became multiples of other rooms because of the dominating grid, which Dawood had chosen and from which he did not deviate. In Makiya's opinion, the grid had become antagonistic to the architecture that it was purporting to help create, and it had resulted in a design in which, in Makiya's view, all the columns were in the wrong place.

Mohamed's son, Kanan Makiya, who was a site architect in the Bahrain office at the time, was devastated at the way Dawood was berated, and decided then that he would never design jointly with his father in the future; instead, he became an administrator of the firm. Following the incident, Kanan and his father had an explosive row about how Makiya could treat in such a belligerent way people who respected him and admired his work – whereupon Makiya collapsed to the floor. A doctor was called and reassured the family that there was nothing wrong. To this day Kanan carries deep feelings of regret that his relationship with his father was never quite the same after that incident as before.

Other architects who worked for Makiya Associates in London from the early 1980s, including Zina Allawi, Mohammad-Reza Daraie, Godfrey Heaps and Garry Martin, were also subjected to Makiya's outbursts. According to Kanan, 'His first reaction was to just look at a design and rip it apart, even if he later accepted it. He was very opinionated and quite intolerant with the architects who were working under him. His implacable, one-dimensional view of anything related to architecture was something they had to live with – or leave. When Makiya realised he was behaving unreasonably, often expecting his employees to know instinctively what he wanted, he would apologise, invite them for lavish meals and act as if nothing had happened,' Kanan said.

The third major problem associated with the now large and growing firm was Makiya's unwillingness to accept that the conceptual side of the design process had at some point to stop, allowing a project to move to the next stage of detailed design. He was often oblivious to the consequences for others of the decisions he made. On the Kuwait State Mosque (1976–1984), for example, he changed the grid at the last minute. The mosque was a massive project with complicated, coordinated drawings from structural engineers, electrical engineers, plumbing engineers and other consultants, all of which had to be changed at a moment's notice.

And as the projects were much larger than those of an earlier era in Iraq, Makiya was not doing his own drawings; whole teams of architects and engineers were now involved. But Makiya had a hard time adjusting to this reality. He would often blame the project architect as the effective team leader – and he frequently did. His sketches were very difficult to interpret and were a continual source of contention; and he invoked aesthetic or architectural arguments that resulted in a poorer quality of working drawings. It became harder and harder to coordinate all the drawings on a particular

Makiya with his team in London, 1980s (Pic: Makiya archive)

project. Anomalies cropped up, and the ensuing problems had to be solved by the architects on site.

Zina Allawi, a soft-spoken woman whose quiet voice and modest demeanour hid her nerves of steel, was given a managerial role at Makiya Associates after Kanan had left, which she combined superbly with her role as an architect. After migrating to London from Iraq, where she had completed her studies in architecture at the University of Baghdad, Allawi worked for a number of British companies. She had just left a job and saw an advertisement for a position with Makiya Associates in the *Architecture Journal*. She decided to apply, but during the interview with Makiya and Kanan she insisted she did not want to be hired just because of her past association with the family. (She had been one of Hind's classmates.) She was very happy with the work after a three-month trial period in 1982 and stayed with the firm until it closed in 1988.

Allawi eloquently described to me the problem of employing high-powered managers. 'They couldn't cope, because you had to understand Dr Makiya. His attitude towards design is up and down – he is passionate. They employed a manager and then they sacked him and employed another one. You have to understand Dr Makiya, his culture and the way he thinks, to be able to work with him. There is no rigid structure. A lot of people were frightened of him. One girl refused to have a meeting with him because of his temper. He would have a tantrum, but she could not understand that it was not anger or malice or hatred. It was the frustration of trying to express his design through the work of other people.'

Zina recalled that, one day in the office, Makiya screamed at her: 'You are an organiser and a manager – come and manage me, come and organise me.' After bursting out laughing she said, 'Dr Makiya, you are just impossible to manage.' She goes on, 'And he also started laughing. Some people get angry because they have hatred, but he is not like that at all – he is a very kind person. A soft person. When things don't get done the way he wants them done, he explodes. He can't cope with people who are slow. He wants people to always be on the go and to match his inexhaustible reservoir of energy and inspiration.'

Zina's administrative skills did not convince Makiya of the need for organisation. 'I remember he was going to give a lecture with [only] a bundle of papers. He said, "Put some structure to this. How am I going to give a lecture?" I started with an introduction, and he said, "This is too organised. I will say what I want to say." You organise him and he puts it aside and does what he wants to do and says what he wants to say.'

The Bahrain and Muscat offices also suffered. Both Margaret and Kanan were very concerned about this and brought it to Makiya's attention, but he always avoided difficult issues if they were not design-related. He would back away from human relations issues, client problems, problems with his staff and problems with office managers.

Bayt Greizah: restoration and extension of an old, two-storey, double-courtyard residence in Oman (Pic: Mohamed Makiya Archive, courtesy of Aga Khan Documentation Center, MIT Libraries – AKDC@MIT)

Conservation of Muscat

Despite these difficulties, the work in the Gulf continued apace. Makiya played an important role in the modernisation of Oman: the oldest independent state in the Arab world, one of the more traditional countries in the Gulf region, and until 1970 one of the most isolated. After deposing his father in 1970, Sultan Qaboos bin Said opened up the country; he boosted spending on health, education and welfare, and he was eager to see rapid development. He also wanted to preserve the unique traditional architecture of the country.

The British Foreign Office was aware of Makiya's work and influenced the Sultan's decision to award Makiya Associates a contract for the conservation of the old town of Muscat. Makiya was appointed a consultant city planner for Muscat. As in Baghdad, he prepared measured drawings in Muscat and drew street elevations with the intention of conveying this remarkable city's forms and outlines to future builders. It was the first time Makiya got a major city-planning job – most of his commissions were buildings – and he was very happy with the work. As in Bahrain, he respected local architectural styles and tried to work within them.

In an article in the *International Journal of Advanced Research*, Dr Soheir Mohamed Hegazy described how 'Makiya defined Muscat as a cul-de-sac city, an enclave of historic buildings that should be kept untouched. . . . [T]he tremendous national value of Muscat's heritage. . . should be enriched by maintenance and renovation. Integration between the old town's fabric and any modernizing scheme should be taken into consideration.'[4]

The Muscat office evolved into one of Makiya's largest offices, employing fifty people in the mid-seventies and bursting with projects. Much of the work involved the renovation of old, traditional buildings and restoring them to their former glory.

Makiya's important projects in Muscat included the renovation of the old city gate of Bab Waljat (1974), Bayt Greizah (1976), and Bayt al-Khyarjiyah (1977) and the new Ministry of Finance, Bayt al-Maliyah, completed in 1977. Tom Wells, who worked as a site manager on one of Makiya's projects for Taylor Woodrow, one of the largest house building and general construction companies in Britain, described his working methods as 'very chaotic'. Wells told me: 'Makiya would change his mind a lot. In the end, Bayt Greizah was completed, but with a lot of help from the contractors. Makiya had a stack of Polaroids of the original building's detail, which he produced on site and which served as the only detailed information provided to the contractors. The project was very successful and remains as it was built in 1976.'

According to Salma Samar Damluji's book *The Architecture of Oman*, Makiya thought that the best way to conserve a traditional urban fabric was to establish 'a vocabulary of design' that would include all the component elements, such as windows and arches. 'It would be very simple,' he said when interviewed by Damluji in

October 1996, 'and it would encourage people to commission and execute their own restorations.' Damluji reports that, 'His idea is to teach local craftsmen "to build in the original vernacular style, and to supply them with facilities and reasonably priced materials so that they can construct their own villages." [. . .] Makiya's thinking was that building comes out of the people and the environment, rather than out of the often unsympathetic, overtly academic approach that architects tend to employ.'[5]

Makiya had an ardent, magnetic personality that impressed friends and clients alike, but he was not a good judge of character. This was very evident in his choice of manager for the Oman office, an Iraqi named Baqir, who had an Iranian background and supported the Iranian revolution.

Makiya also hated handling financial matters and often did not even manage his own bank account. He trusted Baqir with the office bank account, until the man turned out to be a complete charlatan who absconded to Iran with the office's resources. Makiya seems at this point to have had a nervous breakdown, which was a closely guarded secret. His wife, Margaret, saved the day. She came to Oman, calmed and reassured the staff, dealt with clients, and gave her husband the unquestioning support he needed during one of the most difficult periods of his life. The Bahrain office then gradually took charge of projects in Oman.

A decision was taken to establish an office in London serving the main office in Bahrain, and in 1974 the Makiyas bought a property, 11 Sloane Court West, which served both as an office and as a residence for Mohamed and Margaret. The family lived on the upper floors, and the ground floor and basement were for the architectural practice. The brick building with white doors exuded an unpretentious affluence. The exclusive Sloane Club was just around the corner, and the Rose and Crown, a traditional English pub, was at the end of the street. At first London was purely a base for services, with the main office remaining in Bahrain. But, as Makiya spent more and more time in London, it gradually became the central design office as well.

In a video interview with her grandson, Naseem, Margaret recalled: 'It was quite a big difference coming back to England. Things had changed so much in the period I had been away. For example, I had never seen a really big supermarket – that was something new. It was possible to make the adjustment. My husband had to adjust to a different way of working. [. . .] I was offered in the mid-1970s a fellowship at Oxford, St Anthony's College, which I did not take. This was followed by an offer of quite an interesting job in the Saudi embassy, guiding some of the students who came here to study. At the time I thought I would not be able to do that and help in setting up the office, and I didn't take the job. I have since come to regret it because, having worked all my life in Iraq, I [missed] working. I missed the discipline and the whole routine and rhythm of work and also the heightened pleasure of those days when you are not working.'

Having returned to England, Margaret missed Baghdad, and she would speak about her twenty years there as the happiest of her life. When she left England she had been essentially disowned by her father, an overpowering and domineering character, for marrying Mohamed, and she had visited her home town only once, in 1956 for her mother's funeral, before her return in 1974. Whenever Iraqis called Mohamed at home in London and Margaret answered the telephone, she would always say 'Hello' in Arabic. She had mastered the Iraqi dialect and loved to speak it. It was one of the ways in which she kept the memory of Iraq alive for her.

Throughout the rest of her life, Margaret was afflicted by a bipolar disorder.* The cycles of depression that had begun in the mid-1970s gradually got worse, and throughout the 1970s she took various medications. Kanan was the only family member in whom she confided, and it was he who accompanied her to appointments with various psychiatrists, who merely prescribed drugs: there was no

---

* Bipolar disorder is characterised by marked mood swings, ranging from extreme highs (mania) to extreme lows (depression). Episodes of mania and depression often last for several weeks or months.

therapy or discussion of her problems. She was treated with lithium, a drug whose horrendous side effects were then little understood. Kanan got her off this drug in the mid-1980s, when he realised what it was doing to her body and her personality.

Like most Middle Eastern men of his generation, Mohamed Makiya could not understand the phenomenon of depression and seemed oblivious to his wife's plight. Kanan is convinced that Margaret's rupture from her mother and father had affected her deeply; it was not a coincidence, he felt, that her bouts of depression began after her return to the UK from Iraq. In any case, the cycles of depression marked the beginning of a slow unravelling of her relationship with her husband, which had been very strong throughout their marriage, when she was his backbone. Margaret had helped Mohamed write his PhD dissertation, and she assisted him with his talks, and with his papers and other published works. In 1974, when the depression finally kept her from being able to do intellectual work, Kanan had to step in and help. He remembers these as some of the darkest years of his life, made worse by the escalating fights with his father.

Margaret was not happy with the 11 Sloane Court West set-up; the home and office combination was not working as she had imagined. Kanan found a solution to the problem. In 1977, he convinced his father to relocate the office, and discovered a perfect building for Makiya Associates to move into: 26 Westbourne Grove in West London. Although in a dilapidated state, the building had considerable character and a long history. It was one of the earliest built in Westbourne Grove, originally intended as a Shakespearean theatre sometime in the 1860s; it was of an Italianate style, with arched windows and entrance. Most interestingly, it was decorated with portrait roundels between arches, depicting Queen Victoria and Prince Albert in addition to several Shakespearean actors.

As the office moved to Westbourne Grove, Mohamed and Margaret decided they no longer needed such a large property to live in. They moved to Wychcombe Studios, artists' studios that had been converted into town houses in Belsize Park near Hampstead, another upmarket area. Makiya and Margaret bought No. 6, and Kanan and his Iranian wife, Afsaneh, bought No. 5, where their first child, Bushra, was born. (Politics had brought Kanan and Afsaneh together in 1970: she was fighting against the Shah, and Kanan was a revolutionary socialist, with close ties to other revolutionaries in countries of the Middle East.) The town houses with their stained glass windows had a mysterious, old-world atmosphere. Having been born in a traditional Baghdadi house, Mohamed was happy to live in another traditional environment in England.

'We moved several times, which is always a big upheaval in life, but things worked out all right in England towards the end,' Margaret recalled in an interview recorded by Bushra. 'It was nice to see people I had not seen for many, many years. But it was unfortunate, because I was dogged by several bouts of depression, and I don't know why. Nobody understands depression: is it chemical or psychological? That was my worst misfortune during my life in England.

'It was quite a pleasure to be able to watch some of the programmes on British television, which in those days were very good. Radio was good, and there was plenty of access to books, to periodicals, to magazines... But life in the Middle East had been much more leisurely, because of the fact that there was service [assistance with housework]. Service and leisure, the two biggest boons in life, are the two things that are the most difficult to find in the Western environment – not impossible, but difficult.'

Margaret had fond memories of Wychcombe Studios, which were built around a central garden. While her husband continued working on projects in the Gulf and, later, in Iraq, her own life slowed down – but during a period of frantic activity caused by her bipolar disorder, she bought a Swiss chalet. Her husband indulged her whims, and Kanan was left to curb her manic bouts of unreasonable spending when he was in London.

It took a year for Westbourne Grove to be refurbished so that Makiya Associates could use it as an office. During that time the firm rented an annex in the old town hall in Chelsea. New Zealand-born

Godfrey Heaps – a polite, softly spoken, analytical, deep-thinking man who joined the firm as a draughtsman architect – said: 'The two top floors were refurbished initially and were used as our offices. Dr Makiya's office and a conference/reception suite were developed over 1983–84, and the bookshop, design studio and gallery areas were developed later.'

Arab League headquarters

'I was very innocent at twenty-seven,' Godfrey Heaps admitted in interview with me. 'This was my first proper job. And Dr Makiya gave me the responsibility for designing the competition submission for the Arab League headquarters based in Tunis. Zina Allawi and I worked on it together. It came to a crunch at one stage, when Dr Makiya was going away and we had to give him a design to approve for presentation. We did, and got blasted for it. "This is not what I want. What have you done to me? You have destroyed my design, you have destroyed my career," he cried.

'We had to get something new together before the end of the weekend, before he went away. So it was agreed I would come into the office in Westbourne Grove. That was the best experience I ever had with him. He sat with me through the whole weekend. He sketched and I drew, and we produced the design and won.

'Up until then, in my experience, Makiya had been very classical in his architectural language, particularly when designing public buildings. Such designs were typically organised with a modernist's respect for the structural grid, classical and ordered. This was the first building where he seemed to develop in a different direction – inspired, I think, by some of the more random geometries of indigenous architecture. The building we designed had two components: a large cubic structure with grand openings, loggias and incisions that housed the assembly chamber, along with a number of grand meeting and retiring halls; and a second building for administrative staff, including a large suite of offices for the Secretary General. This second building had a large roof supported on two sides by six floors

Makiya Associates and Architecture in Exile

Rashid University in Erbil (Pic: Stephen Kite)

of offices and open on the other sides to views facing the assembly chamber and the city. This great roof was a shade structure, and it protected a stand-alone building for the Secretary General as well as a complex arrangement of courtyards on various levels.'

Heaps describes Makiya as both a boss and a friend. 'We had wonderful times. He was frequently inviting us to a party at his house or to lunch locally. He was very sociable and always keen to celebrate a birthday or an anniversary with an extended lunch at the local Turkish, Iranian or Indian restaurant. If it was a very special birthday, we could find ourselves at the Oxford and Cambridge club or a smart Mayfair brasserie. He was someone whose point of view and enthusiasm for design demanded huge respect. I recall that weekend working on the Arab League headquarters as a very special time for me in my development as a designer.'

Heaps believes Makiya never drew a precise architectural drawing of any of his buildings. 'He sketched a great deal, and we all speculated on how to turn those sketches into buildings, with greater or lesser success. I suspect that this process was very frustrating for Dr Makiya. He could never say something was exactly how he wanted it to be – or perhaps he even felt that no building design was ever completely his own.'

Rashid University

Another important project was Rashid University in Erbil, in northern Iraq (1981–86).

Heinle, Wischer und Partner in Stuttgart, who specialised in university design, won the bidding, but on the condition that Makiya Associates would be the local designer and partner. Mohamed's firm was therefore appointed design advisor for the university, which would cater to 10,000 students. Makiya transformed Heinle, Wischer and Partner's design, introducing courtyards and arches in accordance with traditional spatial concepts, and highlighting brick facades with embedded coloured ceramic tiles, paying homage to both Babylonian and Islamic architectural heritage.

Stephen Kite, an architect on the Erbil project, commented that Makiya Associates' London office in those days had a very pleasant ambience. 'Makiya was an educator as well as an architect,' he told me. 'On the one hand he had to have a commercial office, but it had the atmosphere of an atelier. I think he actively tried to cultivate the feeling of a design studio, such as one has in schools of architecture. We worked on the top floor, which was an open studio. On the lower levels, Dr Makiya had his library. You don't normally see beautiful books in an architect's office. Moreover, the Al Saqi bookshop was there. I liked the whole sense of culture of the place.

'Although Makiya could get angry and frustrated with his team, I remember his essential humanity. My son was born in 1984, when I was working in the Westbourne Grove office, and I felt perfectly relaxed taking my newborn son to work to show him off to my colleagues. Like most Middle Eastern people, Makiya was not at all intimidated by young children coming into the office. Indeed, there was a very Middle Eastern aspect to this fusion of family values, scholarship and seriousness.'

Zina Allawi echoed Kite's sentiments: 'It was like a family. There was no line between work and friendship. There was no clarity that these are the working hours and these are the social hours. The atmosphere was magical – it was not an office. I had up to that point worked for a good seven years in two British offices. There was no emotion. I went in there, I did my work, and I went home. Sometimes, if there was a lot of work to do, I worked overtime. With Dr Makiya it was like a school. We were grown people in our late twenties and early thirties, and it took me back to my high school days, to my student architectural days.

'For a competition we used to stay all night long in our office. My mother used to stay up with me all night long – she helped me make models. I said, "Mum, this is like architectural school all over again. I can't come home, I am working, I have to work." We used to do reports in the middle of the night. Garry [Martin]'s fiancée, an Armenian whom he met in Makiya's office, was typing away. She was a very bright and vivacious woman. We were working on architectural reports through the night. I would write and she would type. It was more of a way of life than a job. There was a passion for work, for getting the best design, for getting the work done.

'There was a competitive atmosphere that is rarely there any more. That was Makiya's personality. He made you love what you are doing, and you could pour all your heart and soul into it. I love cooking, for instance. Whenever there was an event at Makiya's, there was *dolma* [stuffed vine leaves], I used to make those big pots in the traditional Iraqi way. "You skipped a generation, Zina," Dr Makiya used to say. "You are like my grandmother. Who taught you to do this in London?" I have his little note in my files thanking me for this tower of *dolma* I made for one of the office parties. I had to feed the whole office.'

There were also evening symposiums in the office. In 1984 Mohamed gave an inaugural speech to the Royal Institute of British

Architects about Middle Eastern architecture, titled 'Arab Architecture Past and Present' – delivered in conjunction with a special exhibition on Middle Eastern architecture opened by the Duke of Gloucester. Wychcombe Studios, where the Makiyas lived, became a place for parties. The Makiyas had a wonderful Egyptian cook, Muhammad, and Margaret was herself an excellent cook. Her husband loved food, he loved socialising, and he loved talking.

Mohamed embraced London life: he was everywhere. Sometimes life resembled a situation comedy involving two drivers, Eugene and Duggy, who worked for the practice. Makiya would ask one driver to bring knick-knacks or files and folders from the office to the house; Margaret would then ask the other driver to return them to the office.

It was not always easy for architects sitting in London to connect with the Middle East. In a profile of Mohamed Makiya published in *Middle East Construction*, Neil Parkyn noted that:

> [T]hinking your way into a Middle East design problem while working in West London was not easy despite the excellent kebabs and shawarmas on offer outside, but the continuous process of question, solution and refinement which marked the Makiya office generated buildings which responded to their particular settings, or in some cases created new settings of their own. This happened with an international hotel proposed for Deira in Dubai, where Makiya moved from a bold composition of geometric vertical and horizontal forms for the hotel itself to the reworking of the whole waterfront environment. He argued that the prime location of the hotel site at the head of Dubai Creek demanded an appropriate scale in its building.

Mounting a fine Victorian staircase at Makiya's Office in Westbourne Grove, it was immediately obvious to visitors that they were entering the world of a scholar, and a busy one at that. Fragments of decorative tile, calligraphic reliefs and pierced masonry screens took possession of the landings and lobby. At the rear, a former ballroom was converted to accommodate the

Kuwait State Mosque (Pic: Mohamed Makiya Archive, courtesy of Aga Khan Documentation Center, MIT Libraries – AKDC@MIT).

seminars, discussions and encounters which occupied a central place in the work of Makiya and his office.[6]

Kuwait State Mosque

Between 1977 and 1981, Makiya's firm designed and built one of the largest mosques in the world at the time, the Kuwait State Mosque, at a cost of KD 14 million ($46 million in USD) – 130 times the cost of the Khulafa Mosque. Makiya Associates won the contract through an international competition and had three months to finalise the design. It was one of the greatest opportunities in Makiya's career – and it was the first major project won by the new London office set up by Kanan Makiya in 1975.

The Kuwait State Mosque was a radical departure from Mohamed Makiya's previous work. His desire to work with concrete dated back to his student days, when he was influenced by Adrian Stokes's *The Quattro Cento: A Different Conception of the Italian Renaissance*. The phrase 'homage to Mediterranean stone' was pencilled in his handwriting on the inside front cover of his copy.

Elsewhere in the margins of the same book, these words were written: 'What about concrete as stone with living texture and varied coexistence? Why is concrete so insulted by users? Need poetry of architecture to make concrete blossom with life.' Kanan comments: 'These words written in 1944 presaged Makiya's deepest aspirations for the use of concrete in 1977.'[7]

In spite of his inexperience, Kanan put together a team whose goal was to try to re-create the aura of the Islamic past and its elusive spirit, so that a foreign multinational contractor, thinking only of his profits and with no knowledge of Islamic architecture or traditions, could execute the intentions of an Iraqi architect working out of London, 5,000 kilometres from the site. The best and the worst Gulf architecture of the 1970s and 1980s were produced under such impracticable conditions.

The mosque, one of Kuwait's most treasured landmarks, is in a prominent location in the central business district, next to the Seif Palace near the stock exchange. Its construction coincided with a major renewal project of the centre of Kuwait City. The site engineers were Akram Ogaily's firm, Archicentre.

Everything about the mosque is staggering: the building covers 20,000 square metres (220,000 square feet), and 7,000 male worshippers can be accommodated in a 5,000-square-metre prayer hall which lets in natural light through 144 windows. Teak wood was used for the doors. Women have a smaller prayer area that can hold 1,000 worshippers. The external walls are made up of a series of intermediate bays between the main load-bearing structures. Gates of rare wood lead visitors into the complex.

A special room was constructed for the amir. It is accessible from the main prayer hall and is used twice a year by the ruler and his guests. It was designed with symmetrical lines on the ceiling and walls and remarkable hand-carved gypsum ceilings.

Four magnificent chandeliers hang from the central dome, which is 43 metres (141 feet) high and 26 metres (85 feet) in diameter and is decorated with *al-Asma' al-Husna*, the ninety-nine names of God from the Qur'an as designed by the famous calligrapher Muhammad Haddad. The words form a geometric pattern. Calligraphy also decorates the *mihrab*. A copper crescent is placed on top of the dome.

In one respect Makiya kept to the conventional Islamic architectural style in the mosque, adopting a rectangular plan. A patio separates the prayer hall from the main open court to the south. It provides worshippers with a quiet environment for prayer and meditation. A 350-square-metre library houses Islamic reference books and documents.

The interior of the mosque today is decorated with gold leaf, saturated blue, and ornamental calligraphy. Andalusian tilework brightens up the space. The tiles and much of the ornamental work in the interior were added on the instructions of the amir, who felt that the original design was too austere. He unleashed a team of unsupervised Moroccan craftsmen onto the interiors. The result was an explosion of colour that has delighted guidebook writers, though opinions vary. Some love the additions, while others, like Kanan, see them as gaudy Islamic cliché plastered onto the lovingly modelled and nuanced surfaces, giving the impression of a cheap Tangiers hotel.

Underneath the eastern courtyard is a five-level car park which can hold up to 600 cars. The brief for the mosque's design was for the 'Kuwait State Mosque and Multi-Storey Car Park'; no wonder, since Kuwait city is organised around the ubiquity of the automobile, and public transport is virtually non-existent. The incongruity of a Grand Mosque located atop a multi-level car park was not lost on the designers. However, to mitigate the contradiction, the uppermost level of the car park was turned into an extension of the *sahn* (outdoor courtyard), thereby augmenting the scale of the mosque while respecting the brief. The car park was also used as needed to accommodate any sudden influx of more worshippers, particularly during Ramadan.

In *Post-Islamic Classicism*, Kanan questioned the success of Makiya's attempt to give the much-maligned concrete material a life of its own:

If concrete is going to 'blossom with life' its colour must be just right. Imagine a drab grey rose! Concrete blooms on site, not in the studio where airbrush techniques and presentation artistry rule. I managed the studio but made the mistake of ignoring the practical problems of working on site. Alabaster white was the intention and we hoped to achieve this by using special aggregate and white cement in place of grey Portland cement. In the cost-cutting exercise after the tenders came in, white cement was deleted from the specifications. It seemed so simple; 1 million Kuwaiti dinars were saved. The contract was signed. But the consequences were enormous. There are times when the whole world collapses into the colour of a thing. . .

Cynical professionals, with many years of working in the Gulf, were in charge of the contractual negotiations. Architectural intentions went by the board. If the concrete went drab grey or dirty white, some panels turned a sickly pale yellow. No one knows why. Makiya's carefully imagined 'reconstructed stone' (office jargon he invented for concrete), bush-hammered, sandblasted, cast and carved surface finishes, and all the various precast elements (arches, crenellations and panels) had turned into a wild cocktail, a potpourri of finishes. Something had gone terribly wrong.

Despite these shortcomings, Subhi al-Azzawi has nothing but praise for the Kuwait mosque. 'To me, Makiya's best mosque is the State Mosque of Kuwait,' he told me. 'It is a whole mosque, beautifully detailed. Makiya reinvented the wall bay unit as a building element, which was taken from traditional Islamic architecture, and he repeated it everywhere with obviously minor variations. He used concrete and also brick and he used Arabic writing – Kufic lettering. The mosque has a geometric pattern: it is a square with a middle square with four squares in the corners and four rectangular units. It is a masterpiece in terms of planning [and in terms of] its concept, space creation – expressing space in structure as well as unifying space itself.'

Between 1974 and 1981, Kanan successfully managed Makiya Associates, whose projects were almost exclusively centred on the Gulf states. With one exception, a low-cost housing project competition for Baghdad, he did not produce desings of his own, as he increasingly felt he could not relate to monumental commissions of the kind that Makiya Associates was being asked to do. He had a totally different view of architecture from that of his father. Nevertheless, his role as an administrator continued to mitigate conflicts within the office.

But just as the Kuwait Mosque was nearing completion, Mohamed Makiya had a totally unexpected commission. Ironically it derived from the attention Kanan's low-cost housing design had attracted in Baghdad. He was invited back to Iraq in 1980 by Saddam Hussein to help reshape Baghdad for the Non-Aligned Nations Conference in 1982. The decision to go back (described in the next chapter) was one of the most difficult of his life, and resulted in a temporary estrangement from his son, Kanan. When his father began to deal with the Baathist regime, Kanan decided it was no longer possible for him to continue in his role at Makiya Associates. He was starting research on a book, *Republic of Fear*, about the atrocities of the regime, which became a best seller in 1991 after the Iraqi invasion of Kuwait.

In 1980, when Kanan told Mohamed he was leaving the office altogether, his father did not believe him at first. It was agreed that Kanan would find someone to replace him and train his replacement for a year. That person was Australian-born Garry Martin, an experienced archaeologist and art historian as well as a practising architect, who was eventually able to define those elements and qualities in the traditional buildings of the Middle East that were relevant to the design problems Makiya Associates was dealing with.

Martin had graduated from the University of Melbourne in 1968 and in 1969 travelled to England, where he lived and worked until 1989. As an architect and archaeologist, he took part in excavations in Iran, Jordan, Afghanistan and India. An artist who worked for the Makiyas thought that Martin had a lot in common with them, and Kanan invited him to meet his father.

Recalling his meeting with Mohamed Makiya, Martin spoke about sitting on a couch with him, and after three hours of intense, wide-ranging conversation having the feeling of 'coming home' to where he belonged, designing modern buildings in traditional environments. Kanan was relatively quiet during the conversation and seemed to be silently assessing how Martin and his father got along. The next day, Martin was invited to work with Mohamed on the competition for a new government headquarters building in Baghdad to house the Arab Baath Socialist Party and be its flagship building in Iraq.

Martin had only three to four weeks to gather a team, work the design through with Mohamed, and develop his sketches into final presentation drawings. It was the time of Charles and Diana's wedding, in July 1981.

Martin's team worked day and night; Kanan explained that morally speaking he could not contribute to the project, and withdrew completely while the work was going on. The drawings were completed after several all-night sessions and sent away. 'A week later, Kanan called me and we sat and talked,' Martin recalled. 'He offered me the position of co-equal director of Makiya Associates with both of us running the practice for an interim period. Dr Makiya was to be the designer of all projects, and Kanan and I were responsible for the successful running and management of the practice.'

Martin was ideally suited to the director's job. He distanced himself from his boss's mood swings and tantrums and ran the business, leaving Mohamed free to unleash unfettered creative energy on numerous projects, ranging from opulent palaces, state mosques and parade grounds to housing complexes and markets.

But it was not all smooth sailing. Martin admits that he kept a bottle of whisky in the office for when Makiya had furious arguments with the designers; they often needed a drink after such encounters, which were frequent. While he worked for Makiya, betwen 1981 and 1988, Martin was very skilfully able to calm his boss's temper – and to get points of view through to him. Eventually Makiya would agree with these reasoned arguments and work could be finished.

'My role was to ensure that the practice delivered the goods on every occasion. I believe that if he had had someone to mediate and to bring to rest his endless design variations in his earlier years, he would have been one of the world's greatest architects. He hated commitment to a finished design and always wanted to keep changing it, often during construction as well. I understood his feelings and worked successfully with him to commit design to paper and achieve deadlines with his submissions.'

Kanan and Martin worked very well together for about a year in the London office. Martin was grateful that Kanan had stepped back, letting him deal directly with Mohamed. After a year, Kanan told Martin that he was moving to the US to finish writing his book about Iraq. The fact that Martin was one of the very few people who suspected that this book was anti-Baath reflected the level of trust they had achieved in their relationship. Kanan returned for directors' meetings two or three times a year, but never came back to work for Makiya Associates again.

꙳

Martin worked for years with Mohamed, redesigning plans and facades. The Rashid University project took up a lot of his time. He would communicate with the Germans in his by-now-frequent visits to Stuttgart. Every six weeks he would fly to Baghdad with a team from Heinle-Wischer to present designs and discuss them with the client.

Zina Allawi was essentially responsible for bridging the gap between Makiya Consultants in London, which had evolved into the main design office of the practice, and Heinle-Wischer, who 'wanted to build, and were more interested in detailed designs and working drawings. I had to bring the two together. It was a massive project. There were over one thousand elevations to be developed, all in brickwork. It needed a special kind of discipline and organisation to help the design through.'

Stephen Kite, now a professor at the Welsh School of Architecture at Cardiff University, also worked on the Rashid University project as part of the design team. Like many Makiya Associates' employees, he got the job by replying to an advertisement.

'I did not have any problems with working on the university, because I felt it was a very worthwhile thing to do. At that time, a lot of architects from Britain were working for Iraq. Some of them were working on air force bases. I felt that working on a university was something that the country needed, and I was very sad when the project did not go ahead, as Saddam Hussein had decided to wage war on Iran rather than build a university.'

Garry Martin emphasised that Zina Allawi was very much in charge of keeping the job on schedule, as Makiya's interest was in quality and getting the design right, and he was less concerned about deadlines. 'He was in charge of the Makiya style, and he knew when to break the rules,' Martin said. When Martin tried to impress Makiya with sophisticated drawings, Makiya told him not to show off. '"I just want simple drawings that are part of the thinking process," Makiya would say.'

The same methodology and intra-office design relationships were used for Salahaddin University in Erbil. A French engineering practice won the competition and appointed Makiya Associates as design advisers. Martin worked with Mohamed to transform the spatial concepts and facades, and Makiya Associates design teams made presentation drawings for the Iraqi government. Martin communicated Mohamed's design sketches to the French in weekly visits to Paris and had to fly to Baghdad every six weeks to make presentations to the client.

'I took the same view of these projects as Dr Makiya,' Martin noted. 'They were both educational institutions which needed to be built regardless of who was running the country, and they would be there for future generations of students. When we won the government headquarters building in Baghdad project in 1981, I had no major issues with working there, as the West and the USA were supporting Saddam Hussein at the time of the Iran-Iraq war. I was never of the view that many countries in the Middle East could be successful democracies in the Western sense, and had the same view as Plato, who put democracy well down in his list of possible methods of governing societies.' Martin's views were totally different from Kanan's, but they never affected their working relationship, or their genuine and lasting friendship.

The Baghdad State Mosque (1983) was Makiya Associates' last and greatest project in Iraq. The debate about whether or not the firm should work for the Baathist regime could be summarised as 'To work or not to work for Saddam?' Mohamed's agreeing to produce a design for the mosque deepened the estrangement between him and Kanan, who busied himself with his anti-Baath book, titled *Republic of Fear* and first published in 1989, while his father worked for the dictator whose regime he was exposing.

&

'My father never said anything when I left [for the US] – neither did my mother,' Kanan recalled. 'My mother knew why I had to leave; she knew these fights between my father and I were tearing me apart. I hated the idea that I was working for Saddam, and I could no longer be in the same room with my father when he was ripping into some unfortunate architect who could not interpret his sketches. To make matters worse, we lived next door to one another.' Kanan sold his flat in Wychcombe Studios and moved with his wife Afsaneh and their baby daughter, Bushra – Mohamed and Margaret's first grandchild – to live in America. Shortly afterwards his parents sold their flat and moved to Bedford Court Mansions in central London, where they lived for the rest of their lives.

CHAPTER 11

The Baghdad State Mosque

'This is for history. It's not for the people there now [the Baathists]. It's got nothing to do with them; they'll be gone. This is for the future.'

In 1980 Saddam Hussein invited internationally renowned architects to participate in one of the grandest architectural competitions ever sponsored in a country of the Third World. Baghdad had become a testing ground for massive urban renewal. The brief was for a state mosque, the jewel in the crown of the whole Baghdad redevelopment programme approved in 1980. A galaxy of famous names received invitations. The project was initiated in 1983, in the third year of the Iraq-Iran war, at a time when it had become obvious that this was no ordinary war, and that Iraq would not achieve its original aims in starting it. Nonetheless, an Islamic revolution across the border had to be fought on many fronts at the same time.

Hussein had ambitions beyond exerting his grip on a single country – and by 1980 a surplus in oil revenues of US$21.3 billion seemed more than adequate to finance a campaign of conquest and reconstruction. On 22 September Iraq invaded Iran, with the covert support of leading American, British, French and Russian politicians and industrialists, who saw both political and fiscal advantages in containing Iran and confining its religious influence to its own side of the Gulf. Two leading Shi'i voices in Iraq were silenced as a prelude to the attack, Ayatollah Baqir al-Sadr and his sister Bint al-Huda, who were hanged. Ninety-seven members of the Islamic Dawa Party were also executed.

Although the war lasted eight years (1980–88), it altered little in terms of territorial gain and nothing in terms of regime change. Iran had in fact used the war to consolidate its Islamic revolution. While Iraq was now the region's most powerful state, in terms of human life and resources, the cost of achieving so little had been colossal.

❧

The new Baghdad State Mosque was intended to symbolise the religious, state and national beliefs of the people of Iraq, and the President, Saddam Hussein, emphasised that the final design should represent 'a leap forward in the art of architecture'. A three-day televised symposium convened by the President, and attended by every available Iraqi professional and senior government official, was held in Baghdad to hear out the architects, debate the entries and announce the results. Quite apart from architecture, the competition was an orchestrated event of national proportions.

Kanan Makiya's book *The Monument: Art and Vulgarity in Saddam Hussein's Iraq* is a study of the interplay between art and politics – of how culture, normally an unquestioned good, can play into the hands of power, with devastating effects. In it the author notes that:

> [I]n its wisdom, the Mayor's office saw fit to publish all the submissions. Minoru Takeyama, a Japanese post-modernist and winner of numerous prizes, had done some homework. He took the circular plan of al-Mansur's original city (of which not a trace is left) as a 'frame' and the plan of the Great Mosque of Samarra as the 'spirit' of a scheme imbued with historical references. These he jammed into one another.[1]

The Spanish architect Ricardo Bofill produced a melange of many Mesopotamian building traditions, organised along a ceremonial axis. The Robert Venturi* solution to the brief consisted of a dome over the courtyard with an interior that was a cross, Kanan commented, between Disneyland and scenery from Douglas Fairbanks's film *The Thief of Bagdad*.

Twenty-two firms were invited to submit pre-qualification documents to the Directorate of Design at the Municipality of the Capital by September 1982. Six firms, including Makiya Associates, were selected from that initial pool to participate in the competition, and had to submit their documents by January 1983.

But when the results were later announced, the President was not happy with any of the designs and required the competitors to come up with a joint design. They were horrified. Venturi left Baghdad in a huff. The other competitors, including Mohamed, got commissions for other projects in the city's massive urban renewal programme.

༺༻

Mohamed Makiya's involvement with the design of the Baghdad State Mosque began with an invitation from the mayor of Baghdad to visit the city. He told Guy Mannes-Abbott, who profiled him in *Bidoun* magazine:

> When it was announced that Iraq would be the site of the conference of the Non-Aligned Movement, the mayor of Baghdad invited me to come back. He said, 'We want to show Baghdad at its glory, and we have millions and millions you could, you know, spend. We asked everyone – they said, 'Well, Dr Makiya is the only one who used to speak about tradition. Why don't you bring him?' So the invitation arrived, and of course I had to

---

* The architecture of Robert Venturi helped redirect American architecture away from a widely practised, often banal, modernism in the 1960s to a more exploratory design approach that openly drew lessons from architectural history and responded to the everyday context of the American city.

refuse it, because Kanan and my wife wouldn't allow it. Then it came again in a very nice way. The ambassador delivered a letter from the president with the confirmation that I was to come as a guest and leave any time without complication.[2]

The Iran-Iraq war started on the last day of Makiya's stay in Baghdad, 22 September 1980.

Mohamed had a meeting scheduled with Saddam Hussein about his plans to redesign Baghdad's riverfront. But on the day of the meeting Mohamed saw an Iraqi aeroplane heading towards Iran ready to bomb it. The war had started.

When his father was in Baghdad, Kanan asked himself how his father could agree to work on Hussein's project to make Baghdad the envy of the Third World's prime ministers, who were coming to the capital for the Conference of Non-Aligned Nations in 1982. Like many a totalitarian leader before him, Hussein had a craving for prestige, and he wanted triumphal architecture.

Saddam Hussein had once prayed in the Khulafa Mosque, and it was said that he was very impressed with the structure. In fact, he went as far as changing the name of the street in which the mosque was located from Jamhuriya (Republic) Street to Khulafa Street. He was also keen to find alternative talent for Baghdad's makeover and did his homework about the mosque's construction. The issue of who had designed the Khulafa Mosque even came up at a Council of Ministers meeting.

Hussein's officials then wrote to Makiya Associates' London office trying to tempt Mohamed into reshaping Baghdad. Saddam was prepared to forget about Mohamed's alleged involvement with the Freemasons, they told him, and to shower him with lucrative commissions. 'The past was forgotten,' a Revolutionary Command Council official told Kanan on the telephone. Makiya was wary, but few architects can resist the chance to follow Christopher Wren and Baron Haussmann and leave a big mark on their capital. And all that really mattered to Makiya was architecture: he was an architect to his bones. He wanted – in fact, you could say *needed* – to build. Everything else was secondary.

&ᴥ&

The Baathists could not have been more attentive when the former exile finally decided, against his family's advice, to return to Iraq. The customs officials at Baghdad airport waved him in and treated Makiya as a VIP.

When he was in Baghdad, Mohamed discussed with Hussein his ideas for the redevelopment of the city. Saddam Hussein asked about the cost, while Mohamed told him why it was important to have palm trees and not eucalyptus trees brought in from Australia. Hussein liked to use knowledge for his own glorification and when Mohamed told him about traditional brick and and mud architecture he listened carefully to his explanation that the Abbasid tradition is brick building.

By the time Makiya got to work on the design for the Baghdad State Mosque, however, relations between Kanan and his father had chilled to a freezing point. Looking back at that period, Kanan ruminated that a project for low-cost housing, including schools and other facilities for Baghdad's poorest districts, may have drawn Saddam Hussein's attention to Makiya Associates. A Lebanese firm had approached Kanan personally about the design aspects of a competitive bid for 3,000 low-cost housing units, and Kanan, tired of doing large monumental projects for clients he did not respect, was happy to help, as the project would benefit ordinary people. But his father's return to Baghdad, and his beginning work on large projects for the regime, was the breaking point between father and son. Kanan and his family packed up their bags and resettled in the USA in 1982.

'The next big fight we had was when my mother and father came to visit us in 1982, nine months after we went to America,' Kanan told me. 'We lived at first in New York. We rented a house, and I spent five or six days showing him around the city. Meanwhile, I had been busy actually writing the first chapters of *Republic of Fear*. I had not said a word to my father about the book, but he saw a draft of the first two chapters on my desk. There was a huge fight, bigger than the Bahrain fight. He was livid that I was working on this kind of project. He accused me of betrayal and abandoning my heritage. He went back to London, and then six or nine months later he wrote me a letter of apology. That was the one and only time that I know of that he ever apologised to anyone.'

☙❧

Mohamed saw the Baghdad State Mosque not only as a mosque but as a cultural centre for the city. He wanted it to be like the Eiffel Tower in Paris – a landmark that could be seen from anywhere in the capital. He insisted that its size and scale should be worthy of a city which once ruled most Arab lands for four centuries under the Abbasids (750–1258 CE). He saw the mosque as an integral part of the Baghdad of the future.

The brief called for the largest continuous indoor prayer hall, which could hold 30,000 people; a female prayer area for 3,000; a daily prayer area for 1,000; and an additional open-air prayer area for 4,000; a library that could hold 100,000 books and 50,000 manuscripts; a teaching institute; and conference facilities, along with accommodations for forty visiting imams, parking for 1,200 cars and 120 buses, and many other things. Makiya was no stranger to designing large state mosques, and he rose to the challenge.

In their design report, Makiya Associates described the Baghdad of the Abbasids as a city of domes, minarets, towering walls and arched gates; shrines and *khans*; *hammams* (public baths); schools (nuclei of Baghdad's present-day universities); and palaces that once resounded to the sounds of tambourines, flutes and harps. It was a commercial centre where merchants from places ranging from China to East Africa could be found.

Makiya was dreaming of this kind of renaissance for the war-ravaged and beleaguered capital. He was delighted that the site chosen for the mosque was on the road to the airport, exactly over the spot where the second Abbasid caliph, al-Mansour, had built his long-lost round city with a mosque at its heart. Makiya chose to show in his design that this fact proved that it must be the right site, because a truly great monument always has as its subject matter the origin and destiny of a city. And he could achieve this communion of past and future only by viewing this mosque as the focal point of a huge development that would re-enact the historical emergence of the golden age of Baghdad under the Abbasids.

The purpose of his design was to create an environment for continuous use, rather than a single showcase monument standing in a vast open space. Baghdad, Makiya was saying – in the report that accompanied the design – should grow around his mosque, which would become its unifying centre. To the east he proposed dense, multi-use development, including offices, hotels and light industry. To the north, municipal and administrative buildings, leisure venue and cultural services. To the west and in the immediate vicinity of the site, he proposed a four-to-six-storey residential development to replace existing low-density housing. And around the *mihrab* in the south, he introduced an artificial lake, supplied from the Tigris by the revitalisation of an ancient canal, to serve as a giant reflecting pool. What was in reality a filthy, silted-up ditch was imagined by Makiya to be an urban green belt meandering through the whole of western Baghdad.

In the Makiya Associates proposal, the site would be surrounded by a 'monumental' boundary wall, with recessed towers and entrance gateways. The mosque itself would be built of reinforced concrete, with precast elements for *riwaqs* (arcades), beams and finishing panels, and aggregates assembled from all of Iraq for use in reconstructed stone and precast finish panels. A main dome 93 metres in diameter would cover the mosque, with twenty subsidiary domes each 24 metres in diameter and twenty-two smaller domes each 7 metres in diameter. Makiya envisaged these domes becoming a landmark in the Baghdad skyline and creating an unmistakable silhouette at dusk. An inner *sahn* (courtyard) would accommodate 4,000 for outdoor prayer, while an outer *sahn* would have ablution fountains and be surrounded by *riwaqs*. There would be cultural pavilions devoted to the arts and culture of various Islamic countries, and a 'wall of cultures' that would convey the heritage of Iraqi and Islamic civilisation in abstract murals by Iraqi artists. The mosque would be surrounded by landscaped gardens inspired by those from around the Islamic world.

'The Baghdad State Mosque in every detail,' Kanan wrote in *Post-Islamic Classicism*, 'represents a very high degree of abstraction of the Abbasid tradition in architecture. There is nothing like it in the past, yet it belongs to the past in a myriad ways and is indubitably modern.'[3] Unity in diversity and simplicity with dignity – the basic characteristics of Arab architecture and Islamic urbanism at their best, as Mohamed saw them – are expressed in the design.

Garry Martin described the design as the fulfilment of Makiya's life's work and evolving design philosophy – in particular, of his approach to marrying traditional architecture and modern design. 'We went together to Baghdad to present the design directly to the President [Saddam Hussein], along with six other world-famous architects. Dr Makiya spoke in Arabic and was later invited to a personal meeting with Saddam. Dr Makiya treated him with the respect reserved for a fused hand grenade, and emphasised that the heritage of Iraq is promoted in the mosque's design. Makiya sweated so much that the President shifted the meeting twice to cooler areas of the palace.'

Meetings about the state mosque took up most of Makiya's and Martin's time, but Makiya took some time to visit the Department of Architecture at Baghdad University, and to go to an exhibition by one of his favourite artists, Shakir Hassan al-Said. He bought several of al-Said's paintings to add to his growing collection of Iraqi art.

A Jordanian architect, Rasem Badran, was in the end declared the winner of the competition, but it was announced that the project would be given to five of the six entrants to work on together in collaboration. Martin met twice with the heads of the other architectural firms and put forward a joint proposal for a fee and a division of work among practices, which was agreed to by the Iraqi government. Nothing further came of this work, however, and the project died a natural death.

According to Martin, Makiya's design with its one-kilometre-high minaret was by far the most appropriate for a state mosque for Iraq. 'I also felt we had no real chance of winning the competition, as the chairman of the judging panel was a fierce rival and adversary of Dr Makiya. Nevertheless, Dr Makiya's design will be recognised in the long run for what it was: a real concept for promoting Iraq's heritage in a modern idiom centred around a state mosque.'

Commenting on Makiya's design for the State Mosque, Khalid al-Sultani, author of *Mohammad Makiya: A Century of Architecture and Life*, believes that Makiya played it safe with a traditional design. 'He designed a mosque with a dome. It was not such a good idea to adopt this approach – I believe in modernity. You have to express an idea in today's context. Venturi reinterpreted the image of the traditional mosque and made something extraordinary,' al-Sultani said.

Makiya Associates won the competition to design the Ceremonial Parade Grounds in Tikrit, north of Baghdad. The project would have cost more than 100 million dinars had it not been cancelled in 1986. As conceived by Makiya, it was, as he said, never simply a parade ground for watching troops pass by (Hussein's original intention), but a whole cultural and civic centre situated at the southern edge of the town on a desert-like site, in a town whose only claim to fame is that it was the Iraqi president's birthplace. 'The result of the design,' Kanan wrote, 'is breathtakingly beautiful and virtually timeless architecture, an architecture that is rooted in Mesopotamian traditions going back at least 4,000 years and yet has somehow become modern, even post-modern in feeling.'[4]

Godfrey Heaps was the chief designer for the contract for the Ceremonial Parade Grounds. He was responsible to Makiya. 'In

Tikrit Parade Ground (Pic: Mohamed Makiya Archive, courtesy of Aga Khan Documentation Center, MIT Libraries – AKDC@MIT)

December 1984, I went to Baghdad to have discussions with the client body, the engineering office of the government responsible for Presidential projects,' he recalled. 'The engineer in charge of the project was Saad Zubaidi, a very charming and urbane man. He had been the client representative on another Makiya Associates project, al-Rashid University in Baghdad, so there was already a well-established rapport between client and architect. The contract for the Parade Grounds had been agreed, and my visit to Baghdad was to present the initial design, visit the site, and establish contact with the local municipality with regard to the supply of services to the site.

'It was a fascinating trip for me. This was my first encounter with the place that had been the catalyst for Dr Makiya's architectural philosophy. I visited all the buildings beloved by Makiya; I saw Samarra and the Khulafa Mosque and got lost in the traditional streets of the city.

'At that stage, Saddam was in a war enthusiastically supported by the West, but at the same time he was rebuilding his city. I was living very close to the site of the Haifa Street development, a grand avenue that Saddam was building with the help of a number of internationally recognised architects. To create this avenue, he had bulldozed through a large area of traditional urban buildings. The bulldozers cut like a knife through this area. You could see buildings with traditionally detailed rooms and courtyards complete with doors, windows, and screens. It was an architect's education in traditional construction in a moment.

'The Parade Grounds were planned on a square site. The parade route cut diagonally through the square separating the presidential aspects of the brief (viewing platforms, entertainment rooms, helicopter landing pads, parking and the like) from the audience. This side of the parade route was defined by monumental walls and gates and linked to a range of community cultural and sports facilities that formed the public foreground to the parade area,' Heaps told me.

Commenting on the use of the wall bay unit, Kanan Makiya wrote in *Post-Islamic Classicism:* 'The Khulafa, the Kuwait State Mosque and the Baghdad State Mosque are connected in many little evolutionary ways. For example: the symbolism of the dome, the thinking behind the *mihrab* and the development of the technique of the wall bay unit into a barrel-vaulted "thick wall" 12 metres deep [in the Baghdad State Mosque].'[5]

Garry Martin recalled a lot of discussion about the Parade Grounds project before Makiya Associates decided to become involved. 'In the end, Dr Makiya transformed the brief into a national museum of Iraqi art and culture, designed as massive, imposing articulated walls and galleries and landscaping and water features as a celebration of Iraqi heritage. "You could hold a parade there now and then if you want to," Makiya said with a tone of sarcasm in his voice. In the end, Makiya Associates withdrew from the project. They were not paid, and they were concerned about Saddam's war against the Kurds in the north of Iraq.'

The Baghdad State Mosque

In the end, both the Baghdad State Mosque and the Ceremonial Parade Grounds in Tikrit were shelved owing to lack of funds, as Hussein's regime diverted all its resources to financing the Iran-Iraq war.

☙❧

Makiya was engrossed in his architectural work, but he always found time in indulge his passion for Arab and Islamic art and artefacts. This took him to auctions at Sotheby's, Christie's and, later, Bonham's. His assistant Diddi Malek, who studied Arabic and Persian at Oxford and during the 1980s was in charge of providing the cultural and heritage background for his projects, was the ideal companion for these buying trips.

'He loved to buy things,' Malek told me. 'He looked at art and architecture – he was a visual person. When he designed the Kuwait State Mosque, he was a great believer in special finishes and geometric and Islamic patterns, and he would use all the nineteenth-century books in his library that had all the geometric patterns. He loved the tiles of fifteenth- and sixteenth-century mosques, and he wanted to incorporate tiles into his designs, along with carved wooded screens [*mashrabiya*]. That is where his love of art came in.'

Unlike many of her colleagues, Malek found Makiya easy to work with, but she admits that he was quite exacting. 'If he saw a design and he did not like it, he would tell his staff. So people in the office were worried about showing him something. They would come to me and say, "We want to show him this – can you show it to him?" When he said something was not good, he was usually right.'

Like many of Makiya's employees and friends, Malek described him as a kind of father figure in the office. 'We were like his big family at work. He taught me a lot. He would say, What are you doing for lunch? I would be meeting a girlfriend, and he would take everybody out for lunch. He would have gone out every single day for lunch if he could. He loved it. All my friends loved Dr Makiya.

They all knew what a great role he played in my life.'

When Malek left Makiya Associates in 1986 to set up the Islamic Department at Bonham's, Makiya would come to all her auctions. 'He loved Matisse. He was looking at all kinds of art, not just Islamic art. He loved Islamic manuscripts. He bought old pots and bowls. It was the artistry of the piece that appealed to him. He was not worried if it had a dent or a chunk taken out of it. I tried to stop him from spending. Margaret was always asking him, "Where are we going to put these things?" and many of them were stored in his office.'

Garry Martin continued working with Makiya Associates until the firm closed in 1988. 'We often travelled together and gave talks at exhibitions and presentations,' he said. 'We had many visits to Paris, Stuttgart, Baghdad, Tunis, the Emirates and Japan. There were many amusing dinners, and we always enjoyed ourselves on our trips together. The design sessions with Japanese designers of a major office building in Saudi Arabia were wonderful. We had no common language except design, and it was amazing how we worked through all the design advice issues successfully, with much laughter and sketching interrupted by banquets and drinks.'

༄༅

Diddi Malek and Mohamed Makiya remained life-long friends. Kanan and his father eventually reconciled, and Mohamed expressed his pride in his son's work in the interview with Lawrence Weschler (who profiled them first in *The New Yorker* and then at greater length in his non-fiction novella *Calamities of Exile*).

Weschler described in detail a meeting he had with Mohamed in his London office. Mohamed showed him the designs of the Baghdad State Mosque and the Tikrit Parade Grounds. When Weschler asked him if Mohamed was glad they were never actually built he first said 'yes' then 'no', and in the end pointed out that the plans were still there and maybe they could be made use of in future.

Mohamed also spoke about his disagreement with Kanan:

'I was so embarrassed when Kanan left the firm, so hurt,' he said. 'I thought that his leaving was for other reasons. I thought, What is he doing over there [in America], just taking care of the children while his wife goes off to work? He's wasting his life. But I was wrong. Because anything that can help bring democracy to Iraq, that's worth a thousand of these.' His gesture took in all the plans on his desk. 'That's what will make thousands of others possible.' Then, jabbing a finger in the direction of a copy of *Republic of Fear* lying on a side table, he said, 'That's the most important thing our family ever did for Iraq.'[6]

CHAPTER 12

The Kufa Gallery and the Sultan Qaboos Mosque

*'The most important thing in our lives is heritage.
We have to take care of it, we have to know about it.'*

By 1986, the lucrative contracts in the Gulf were coming to an end, and the architectural practice was winding down. Iraq was virtually bankrupt owing to the Iran-Iraq war, and many of Makiya Associates' projects in Iraq were not carried to fruition. Makiya's grand ambitions for the Baghdad State Mosque, the Tikrit Parade Grounds and other projects would never be realised.

Nazar Makiya, who ran the UAE Office of Makiya Associates, took upon himself the main responsibility of winding up Makiya Associates. Mohamed's relative Ghassan Makiya, who would go on to establish his own private consultancy in Doha, regrets that Makiya, whom he describes as 'not a business-minded person', did not extend his work beyond the Gulf. He had started working with Mohamed in the late 1970s. Ghassan started some fifteen years later and worked under Nazar (his elder brother) as a site engineer in Qatar. He then stayed on in Qatar to work in a more general capacity under Nazar in Qatar.

In 1988, in London, Makiya took part in his first ever demonstration against Saddam Hussein's regime, responsible for the assassination of the Iraqi religious leader Mahdi al-Hakim, whom he had known and respected. In January of that year, Baath agents had lured al-Hakim to an Islamic conference in Khartoum and murdered him in the lobby of the Hilton Hotel. The Iraqi expatriate community back in London exploded in anger. Marching past the Iraqi embassy, Makiya knew that in all likelihood he was being photographed, and his association with the Baath was thus being irretrievably sundered.

Thereafter he began to allow the Kufa Gallery, which he was running from the building that housed his architectural consultancy, to be used for Iraqi meetings in opposition to the regime, and gradually made a transition: from being a leading architect, he became a leading promoter of Arab culture in London.

☙❧

Kanan Makiya and the Lebanese artist, publisher and activist Mai Ghoussoub were close friends and comrades from the time they had been involved together in various leftist organisations in the 1970s. After the civil war broke out in Lebanon, Ghoussoub, while bringing assistance to refugees in the Palestinian camps, was hit in the eye by shrapnel. When she came to London for medical treatment she stayed with Kanan, who eagerly tried to find a way to keep her active and safe from the turmoil engulfing Lebanon. Out of this friendship the new idea of an Arabic-language bookshop in London was born.

It was called Al Saqi (the water carrier). The logo was adapted from one of Jewad Salim's sketches owned by Mohamed Makiya. It was the first Arab bookshop in London – and in Europe – and a few years later evolved into a Middle East publishing house. Lebanon, hitherto the capital of Arabic and English media culture, was disintegrating into a prolonged civil war. Newspapers moved to London and Paris, and London seemed like an ideal location for the bookshop. In 1977, a company was established with the assistance of Mohamed's lawyers. The shareholders of the bookshop were Mai Ghoussoub, her husband, Jon Rothschild, Kanan Makiya and André Gaspard. Hind was a sleeping partner. The bookshop thrived

Ahmed Shiry painting of the building in 26 Westbourne Grove, London of the Kufa Gallery and Saqi Books, 2002 (Illustration © Ahmed Naji from *Under the Palm Trees: Modern Iraqi Art with Mohamed Makiya and Jewad Selim*, Rizzoli, 2019)

and became a centre of Arab cultural excellence under Ghoussoub's management and with Kanan's behind-the-scenes support.

Starting in the late 1980s, Mohamed began to find a new outlet for his creative energies: the Kufa Gallery. Kufa, on the banks of the Euphrates, has a history dating back to antiquity with roots in

Sumerian culture. It was a gateway to the desert, the destination of many caravan routes, as well as the link between Mesopotamia and the sea, and its green and fertile fields provided nourishment for the enrichment of both body and soul. Originally a military base, it became a leading cultural and religious centre – 'the Athens of the East' – producing the first Islamic calligraphic script and laying the foundations of Islamic legal and theoretical studies. As the tenth-century writer al-Jahiz said, 'If you seek elegance, go to Kufa.'

Makiya chose the name 'Kufa' for the gallery in honour of the university he had hoped to establish in Iraq. In its first years, the Kufa Gallery was run by Mai and Kanan as an extension of Saqi Books, which was in the same building. But as its activities expanded Mohamed felt the need for a more permanent director. He appointed Rose Issa as the gallery's first artistic director. A feisty Iranian-Lebanese woman whose insight into the Arab world derived from having a Lebanese father and an Iranian mother, she had an ideal background to run the gallery. Her childhood was spent in Iran; she graduated from the American University of Beirut with a BS in Mathematics; and she had a command of Arabic, Farsi, English and French. Between 1973 and 1977, she worked for the Iranian Radio-Television Middle East Office in Beirut; she then left for Paris, a few years after the civil war started in Lebanon in 1975, to be with a French archaeologist whom she would later marry.

Through the gallery, Makiya brought the history of Mesopotamia and the Fertile Crescent to the environs of the Thames. In an interview with *Al Aalam* magazine,[1] Mohamed described Kufa as a venue intended as a meeting point for Middle Eastern cultures and the West. 'The aim of establishing it was to show off our Arab presence in the international cultural scene. It is true that each society has its own cultural specificity, but what I see is unity in diversity, and this is one of the secrets of the success of Islam.'

The aim of the gallery as described in its introductory brochure was to generate an understanding of ancient East/West connectedness and put an end to ideas based on division by promoting notions of world citizenship, and stretching geographical and ideological boundaries until they became transparent. Makiya spoke about his hopes that the gallery would promote a greater understanding of the 'global village' philosophy: the concept of *al-Mamoura* first referred to by al-Farabi in the twelfth century and again in more recent times, in the mid-1960s, by Marshall McLuhan.

He also commented to *Al Aalam* that he was changing his role 'from a practising architect to someone who just shares ideas... The other thing that occupies me is I am busy recording what I have gained through my experience and my studies. I want to record these in short notes so they become a useful record for the next generation.'[2]

༄༅

The gallery hosted numerous art exhibitions to promote Middle Eastern art in London. The first Kufa Gallery exhibition in 1986, organised by Mai and Kanan, was an exhibition of Lebanese art generated during its civil war. The second, when the gallery was run by Mohamed and Rose, was on book covers of the Arab world. An exhibition of old Arab and Islamic maps from Makiya's collection followed. In October 1987, an important exhibition was organised to honour and commemorate Naji al-Ali, the famous Palestinian cartoonist who was known for his political and satirical works criticising both Arab governments and the Israeli government. He was shot in July 1987 and died a month later.

The exhibitions were not intended for commercial gain, as the Kufa Gallery was established as a charitable organisation dedicated to furthering research in and knowledge of Arab, Islamic and Middle Eastern culture. The gallery would ask each artist exhibiting to donate one or two artworks to help defray the cost of the staff employed by Makiya directly. Volunteers also helped to run the gallery. This allowed it to become a significant platform to showcase Middle Eastern art on cultural terms not restricted by the art market or the politics of the academic and cultural institutions in England.

Rose Issa worked tirelessly for the gallery for two years, and it quickly became London's premier (and at that time only) venue for exhibitions of Middle Eastern and Islamic art. 'We had the pulse of the Arab world. If you wanted to know about the Arab world, you came to the Kufa Gallery,' Issa told the author.

'I loved Mohamed Makiya,' said Issa, who always speaks about him with great affection, respect and admiration. 'He had the intelligence of the heart and the intelligence of the eye, and he was extremely generous. We never had a problem, because we had a father-daughter relationship, which means you can fight. You can say "no".'

Some of the works of the artists found their way to Makiya's private art collection. Sometimes, when there was an exhibition, Mohamed would want to buy all the artworks, but Issa did not let him: 'I said "no" – you can only acquire two artworks. And if you want to hold an exhibition, it has to come through me.' Issa was one of the few people who managed to stand up to Makiya and insist on her point of view without alienating him or incurring his wrath. 'On Friday,' she recalled, 'he would invite artists, journalists and whoever was in the gallery to an Iranian restaurant for lunch. He had a very generous heart.'

In 1988, Mai Ghoussoub had curated an exhibition of contemporary Lebanese art showing important works by Chafic Abboud, Saliba Douaihy, Paul Guiragossian, Mohammed El Rawas, Ida Allameddin, Fadi Barrage and Fatima El Hajj. The second important exhibition in 1988 featured the work of twenty-four Arab women artists in the UK. The artists were all in the UK, but they did not know each other, and the exhibition enabled them to meet.

Three influential Iraqi artists – Dia Azzawi, Rafa Nasiri and Saleh al-Jumaie – held a group exhibition at the gallery showing lithographic artworks and collages charged with references to Islamic and Mesopotamian heritage. There was also a solo show for Dia Azzawi. 'We sold half of the work,' Issa said. She also organised an exhibition for Etel Adnan, now one of the most famous artists in the Arab world.

Invitation to an exhibition at the Kufa Gallery 1999 (Pic: Ahmed Naji, *Under the Palm Trees*)

There were exhibitions of social life in the Middle East; there were photographs of Kurdistan by Rupert Conant, Julia Bigham, Martin Pope and Nasrollah Kasraian, and a photo exhibition of Basra; and photos of people of the Golan Heights – life under occupation – by Michiel de Ruiter and the Arab Association for Development, Golan Heights. Kufa Gallery was also the venue for a group exhibition of Sudanese and Somali paintings, exhibitions of the artwork of Iranian artist Reza Hosseini, a show of nineteenth-century European paintings of the Middle East, the works of Yemeni artists, and drawings by Iraqi, Yemeni and Palestinian children. There were also exhibitions of Arabic calligraphy, along with a display of old maps of the Arab and Islamic worlds.

☙❧

Makiya became a patron of Middle Eastern art, and for twenty years Kufa Gallery was a meeting point for artists, writers, intellectuals and potential collectors – anyone who had minimal curiosity about the Middle East. In addition to the exhibitions, there were weekly lectures. For twenty years at the Kufa, Wednesday evenings became important dates in the cultural and social calendar of any Londoner interested in Arabic, Islamic or Middle Eastern affairs. Makiya's transcultural experience, architectural practice and environmental

Reflections on the Years

concerns highlighted a need for a public forum where seminars and lectures as well as concerts and exhibitions were open to interested parties from all backgrounds who were as eager to invest in their connected futures as they were to cherish their pasts. (The lectures were coordinated and organised by Rashid al-Khayoun, author of *Reflections on the Years,* the book that recorded memories that Makiya had dictated to him. Makiya understood al-Khayoun to be volunteering his time, but Kanan always made sure he was paid.)

Dr Subhi al-Azzawi lectured on the architecture of oriental houses; Dr Besim Hakim on the Islamic City; Michael Wood on

Iraq and the origin of ancient civilisations in Iraq; Dr Shirley Guthrie on the influence of Arabic literary tradition on the picaresque novel; Professor Nicola Ziadeh on memories and autobiographies in modern Arab literature; Professor Roy Mottahedeh on the role of fate in the *Arabian Nights*; Dr Sami al-Badri on a new interpretation of cuneiform scripts in Mesopotamia; Ali al-Shouk on sketches from the ancient history of Iraq until the fall of Babylon; the late Dr Lamia al-Gailani on Hammurabi and his contemporaries, and on the antiquities market in Iraq; Dr Rifat Chadirji on symbolism in art and architecture; and David Jacobs on the conservation of Islamic manuscripts.

There were also lectures on the philosophy of architecture, and on the castles and mosques of Oman; on saving the heritage of Najaf and Karbala, and on the destruction of the marshlands of southern Iraq; on the humanistic concept in Islam, on the unity of science and art in Islamic geometric designs; and on al-Haram al-Sharif, the Noble Sanctuary in Jerusalem. Emile Habibi, the Palestinian novelist and activist, lectured (on 17 May 1991) on the responsibilities of Arab intellectuals with respect to current events in the Arab World; other activists and writers participated in numerous events highlighting the plight of the Palestinian people.

During the lectures, Mohamed sat quietly among the audience unless he was introducing the speakers, and he often asked questions. He himself gave a number of lectures at the gallery, including on the Kufa University project in the 1960s. Subhi al-Azzawi recalled that he tended to repeat the same two-hour lecture. 'The first time you heard it, it was fantastic. The second time it was OK.'

Kufa Gallery was also a venue for music: musicians from Iraq, Iran, Turkey and, especially, India organised concerts and recitals of modern and traditional music. The ground floor was once a music hall, and the acoustics were superb. Jay Visvadeva wanted an intimate venue for his concerts and loved the Kufa so much that he rented an extension of Makiya's office for his own company. Many British and American people who were great fans of Indian music came to the concerts, along with Indian families. The musicians ironed their white silk robes on the premises.

'When I found out about Kufa Gallery, it became like my second home,' Dia Kashi told me. One of Kanan Makiya's closest Iraqi friends in London, he had met the Makiyas in the 1950s in Baghdad, where his family had an antiques and carpet business, and was overjoyed to find the Makiyas in London. 'I would see Makiya at least twice or three times a week. We became close, especially when I got to know his son Kanan. We became very close friends through Iraqi politics. When Kanan started writing about Iraq, we found out that we had a lot in common.'[*]

☙❧

In addition to the 'home' created by the gallery, where he spent many weekdays when the gallery was first established, Makiya also had a rural retreat, a cottage in the Cotswold village of Upper Slaughter, to which family, colleagues and friends escaped for long weekends.

The cottage started life as a smithy working iron for the local blacksmith sometime in the nineteenth century. It was converted into a rural retreat in the 1950s and bought by the Makiyas in the late 1970s on Margaret's initiative. The family used it as a holiday home and often went to the cottage to get away from their busy London life. Like all the buildings in its secluded village, it is made of stone and has a stone wall around the one-acre property. A winding path leads to the cottage, and red and white roses decorate its walls. Tall, slender bushes rise almost to the roof and strategically display their flowers to the best advantage.

---

[*] During crises, Dia Kashi helped take care of the Makiya family's affairs in London.

The Laurels: The Makiyas' cottage in the village of Upper Slaughter in the Cotswolds (Pic: Roy Coutinho)

The Sultan Qaboos Mosque

Makiya's last architectural project, undertaken when he was running the Kufa Gallery, was the Sultan Qaboos Grand Mosque in Oman. The Sultan decided in 1992 that his country should have a grand mosque rivalling that of Kuwait, which had by now acquired an international reputation. The following year, Makiya, as the respected designer of the Kuwait Mosque, was invited to participate in a competition for its design. He asked Quad Design, founded by Zina Allawi and Godfrey Heaps and other former Makiya Associates architects, to work with him, and jointly they won the bidding in October 1993.

Quad Design had been set up in 1987 and was led by the leading lights in Makiya Associates: Godfrey Heaps, Zina Allawi, Mohammad-Reza Daraie and Essam Amer, a former director. Makiya and Kanan kept in touch with Quad and supported it during its early years.

'We set up Quad Design as we had experience in the Middle East,' said Zina Allawi in interview. 'Five years later, Dr Makiya came with his proposal for the competition for the design of the Sultan

The Kufa Gallery and the Sultan Qaboos Mosque

Makiya in Muscat, 1999 (Pic: Ahmed Naji, *Under the Palm Trees*)

Qaboos State Mosque. That is how we got started in Oman. We already had a number of smaller projects in the UAE from 1987. Now we are one of the leading architectural firms working in Oman.'

As an individual operating from the Kufa Gallery, Makiya worked with Quad on the preliminary stages of the job. He was very much involved in the conceptual thinking, with Quad acting as the executive architects. Makiya would come to Quad's small design and administrative Bloomsbury office in central London and see how the project was developing. The mosque was opened in 2001.

In the 2015 article 'Place of Praise', *The Business Year* observed that the Oman Mosque 'presents a spectacular array of traditional Islamic art and encourages its visitors to interact with the spirit of Islam. This architectural treasure was built over an area of 416,000 [square metres], with the entire pavement surface formed by different types of marble installed in impressive geometric patterns. Aside from marble, the second most important material used in this opulent project is Indian sandstone, with 30,000 tons of it covering the walls and external enclosure of 65,000 [square metres].'

Verses from the Qur'an are etched onto the walls of the courtyard. Unmissable is the gigantic crystal chandelier above the prayer hall, suspended 14 metres below the ceiling. As with the Kuwait mosque, the dimensions of the Sultan Qaboos Mosque are breathtaking. It is divided into four sections: the main prayer hall (*musalla*), which can hold 6,500 people; the women's prayer hall, with space for 750; the library; and a lecture theatre. Outside is a paved area that can accommodate 8,000 people. When the available areas of the inner quadrangle and passageways are factored in, the total capacity is 20,000 worshippers.

Ali Mousawi, one of Makiya's best students, worked in association with Makiya on a university project and kept in touch with his former professor throughout his life. He says that, 'Oman's mosque is a beautiful mosque because Makiya allowed others to take care of the details. He is a master, he is a philosopher. He developed the concept of the mosque. He is a scholar more than a pure architect, but when it comes to details he gets too involved.'

As in Bahrain, Makiya insisted that the mosque design should complement Oman's unique architectural style. 'When I designed that mosque in Muscat, I wanted people to relate to it as a cultural centre. The building went right up to the water, the sea, and the mountain. Because Oman is defined by the rock and the water. And they ruined it by having an 80-metre street passing right by the mosque! To me the mosque is not a place to worship only, it is a place of rendezvous, like a national park. Children could come and play and all that, have a parade, and people could picnic there and all that. Then they could pray if they want to, in the thousands.'[3]

൞

In April 2002, the *Guardian* tracked Mohamed down and profiled his interesting life. 'If you visit the exquisite village of Upper Slaughter in the Cotswolds, with its lazy stream and its famously expensive hotel, you may spot an elderly man with a pipe outside one of the cottages,' Andy Beckett wrote in an article on Iraqi exiles in the United Kingdom. 'He speaks with an un-English huskiness and he favours dark suits and long, faintly Middle Eastern scarves, but Dr Mohamed Makiya is an Anglophile of the old school. He was born in Baghdad, yet he has been a member of the Royal Institute of British Architects since 1948. He holds passionate opinions about Gladstone and Christopher Wren. His London residences, over the decades, have been in Bloomsbury and Hampstead.'

Beckett's article focused on Makiya's career as an architect, his work for Saddam Hussein, and his subsequent break with the dictator. There was no mention of the fact that he had made a smooth transition from being an architect to becoming a patron of Arab art and the driving force behind the Kufa Gallery in Westbourne Grove. Mohamed's rural retreat made it possible for him to play the perfect host in peaceful, cordial surroundings. He was respected and admired in London's intellectual and cultural circles, and he had reached an understanding with Kanan regarding their differing views on politics once they reconciled after their explosive rupture about undertaking projects in Hussein's Iraq.

In truth, Mohamed Makiya had become more and more distressed over the character of the regime he had been associated with between 1980 and 1986. 'In the 1990s, my father entered an increasingly religious phase,' Kanan recalled. That shift toward religion coincided with a shift in the philosophy of the Kufa Gallery, from its secular beginnings in 1986, when Kanan, Mai and Rose were involved with it, to a culturally Shi'i establishment in the 1990s.

Mohamed 'returned more deeply than before to his Shi'i roots,' Kanan noted. 'Visitors began calling on him at home: Shi'i men so observant that they wouldn't even acknowledge my mother's presence, let alone shake hands with her.' Both Kanan and his mother found this deeply offensive.

Rose Issa was the gallery's artistic director and manager from 1986 to 1988. All subsequent directors found it impossible to stand up to Makiya. For Annette Kubba, a British woman married to an Iraqi, it was hard to handle the demands Makiya made on her. He often raided the gallery's files and took away photographs instead of having them scanned. Only Issa could say 'no' to Makiya, and he interfered in the gallery's programming and found it difficult to let the staff do the jobs they were hired to do. But despite these shortcomings, the gallery's exhibitions and lectures continued apace. Everyone wanted to be with Makiya, and he spent too much time socialising to worry about the Kufa's internal problems – which inevitably got worse. The gallery was running at a loss, but Kanan made sure it had enough money to keep going until it finally closed in 2006.

'I frequently went to visit my uncle in the gallery for just half an hour,' Mohamed's niece Amal recalled, 'because he always had some people coming to see him. We would take him for lunch and come back to the gallery. He was happy when the gallery was there. Everyone would go there. His close friends came to see him.'

In 1989, the Kufa Gallery held an important commemorative exhibition for Jewad Salim, who had died in 1963. Salim's wife, Lorna, an artist in her own right, and other prominent Iraqi artists participated: Dia Azzawi, Muhammad Ghani Hikmat and Nuha al-Radi. The photographer and artist Nadhim Ramzi provided rare photographs from his archive. The event was a landmark cultural statement at a time when Iraq was licking its wounds from eight years of war with Iran and an ongoing genocide was unfolding in Kurdistan. The last thing to expect from Iraq at that time was to remember Jewad Salim.

The exhibition still stands unmatched: in its standards, in the level of participation, and in its reception. Lorna Salim showed a masterpiece, *Homage to Jewad Salim* (1989), a pencil, ink and watercolour on paper work. Ahmed Naji told me: 'Her piece depicts a white mosque dome against a transparent beige background that conveys a sense of an ageing and archival atmosphere. In the background, as well as on the neck of the dome, several of Jewad's Iraqi symbols adorn the painting in subtle, white purity. The beige background is filled with the names of Jewad's friends, students and colleagues, all of whom attended and signed the edge of the painting. The painting then acquired more beauty with the signatures of the attendees at and participants in the 1989 exhibition. It is one that Kanan still treasures and which occupies pride of place in his London flat.'

Makiya was always keen to keep records of events at the gallery. He asked professional photographer Hussein al-Sikafi to take photos of the exhibitions and lectures: Sikafi enjoyed the work, but admits Makiya was not an easy person to work with. 'He insisted on perfection and always told me you have to be the best at what you are doing. He had the vision of an artist. He would say, "This is a good picture." One day he saw a picture, bent it in half, and said this picture would make a good post card. He paid attention to everything – to every detail. I always showed him my pictures, and he would tell me how to crop them. He said the camera does not do the work – your eyes do the work.

'He told me to take photos of Portobello market. "They are our neighbours," he said. "There is a relationship between us and Portobello – people there know the value of antiques and architecture."

'When talking about architecture, he used to say, "My roof is the sky. Our spirit looks to the sky." He did not like the idea of enclosed buildings. He did not want to cut the space. He was against sharp edges in buildings. He talked about buildings as if they were human. If somebody banged the door, he would say, "The door is here to serve us; take care of it." For him, everything had life.

'When he was talking about the Khulafa mosque he forgot himself; he forgot about everything and went into the spirit world. I felt like that when he was talking about architecture and art. He could talk for hours and make you aware of the value of architecture and the value of the environment.'

Makiya was the perfect host, welcoming artists and lecturers to the gallery with an engaging smile. He greeted everyone as though he were inviting them to his home. When anybody who worked with him had a baby or graduated or got his or her British citizenship, he made a big party for the occasion, so that everybody in the Kufa Gallery could celebrate. This was, in his view, in accordance with Arab tradition, and he insisted on observing that tradition.

Mesopotamian storyteller Fran Hazelton often went to the Kufa Gallery for theatrical productions of key episodes in the *Gilgamesh* epic. It proved to be a life-changing experience. 'The epic made such an impression on me that I went on to study with Andrew George, who published the definitive translation of *Gilgamesh*. Eventually I told it myself as an oral storyteller. I owe a lot to the Kufa Gallery.

'I don't remember who introduced me to the Kufa Gallery, but I had been going there for some time before I met Dr Makiya. My storytelling group did a whole season of stories from Mesopotamia at the Kufa Gallery. Dr Makiya got suitable pictures of the architecture of the period, which he put on display, and of course it was a wonderfully appreciative audience – mainly Iraqi. They were very kind to us, going there and telling the stories in English. Kufa was a lovely gallery with a very nice atmosphere. Dr Makiya called it a *diwania*. We have this word in English, "divan", which comes from Arabic culture. A divan is a welcoming place where people can come and sit, and they had those sort of benches, like a divan.'

ஓ&ஓ

The famous Iraqi author and journalist Khalid al-Kashtini was also very active at the Kufa Gallery. Kashtini wrote many books, including *Arab Political Humour*, *Arabian Tales*, *By the Rivers of Babylon*, and *Tales from Old Baghdad*. In 2015 he received the best Newspaper Column Award at the Arab Media Forum held in Dubai.

'I presented a few lectures there,' Kashtini recalled. 'I was just a fan going there regularly. It became a centre for the Iraqis, especially enlightened, progressive Iraqis. We did not just go there for the lectures – it was a meeting place. After the lectures we would go to restaurants or cafés. It was in a very good location in the heart of the Arab part of London.'

Over the years, the gallery's focus changed. At first, when Mai Ghoussoub and Rose Issa were its directors, its exhibitions and talks encompassed the whole Arab world and it was a favourite meeting place for London's Arabs. As the directors changed so did the focus, which turned to topics of interest to the Iraqis and than to Shi'i Iraqis. The last director was Walid Khazaraji, a very conservative Shi'i who at first would not shake hands with women. The character of the gallery changed under his management and alienated secular Iraqis.

CHAPTER 13

Conflict and Reconciliation

'I am a conductor without an orchestra.'

By late 1999, Mohamed Makiya's health was in decline, and he was going to the gallery only once or twice a week. 'The gallery was also very costly to run,' Kanan told me, and 'the family could no longer afford the £4,000–5,000 a month it took. We would always disagree about how much things cost. I would tell him the cost of something, and my father would say, "That is far too much." He refused to accept that not everyone was willing to work for nothing. For the last ten years of the gallery's existence, he believed everyone working there was doing so out of love of being there. As he grew older, he became more conscious of money, but without really accepting how the world around him worked. He told me I was always throwing money away because I insisted on paying for services rendered. So finally we made a deal: he would not ask me about the accounts and how much I was paying to whom, and I would not tell him what things cost, including his and my mother's home carers. He was happier not knowing. I made sure Kufa Gallery had what it needed to run: I paid Walid [Khazaraji] enough money to run the gallery and for him to earn a proper salary, and Walid would pay whatever (and whoever) had to be paid. I more or less had the same arrangement with his home carers.'

❧

Meanwhile, during the 1990s, the situation had changed once again in Iraq. When the Iran-Iraq war ended, Saddam Hussein put on a false show of promoting a new level of freedom, promising a new constitution, a multi-party political system and a free press. But at the beginning of August 1990, after a squabble over oil prices and levels of production, Iraq invaded its neighbouring country, Kuwait – just two years after the Iran conflict had come to a close.

The international community responded immediately by imposing sanctions on Iraq; then, on 29 November the UN Security Council authorised 'all necessary means', including the use of force, to restore stability to the area. Attempts at diplomacy achieved nothing, and in January 1991 the Iraqi Parliament resolved to go to war rather than withdraw. A US-led coalition composed of twenty-eight UN member states initiated a bombing campaign on 16 February. After 91,000 air missions had been carried out over Iraq and Kuwait, and a ground campaign that routed the Iraqi army, Iraq accepted a ceasefire on 3 March.

Mohamed couldn't understand why the allies took out the bridges over the Tigris – and most particularly the one key suspension structure, which as an architect he had long prized. He used to ask Kanan what the military sense was in that, pointing out that all it did was to hurt the common people going about their daily lives and deface Iraq's common heritage.

In 1991, there was a public revelation that Samir al-Khalil, the pseudonym of the author of *Republic of Fear*, was really the son of Mohamed Makiya, Kanan. Kanan organised a number of meetings for the London expatariate community and Mohamed attended them all, sitting at the back of the room and puffing thoughtfully on a pipe.

Kanan's argument was that the time had come for a decisive gesture – an acknowledgment of what '1991' had come to mean in the history of Iraq and some codification of a vision of the future. He envisaged a charter which he called 'Charter 91' in honour of its Czech antecedent – Václav Havel's Charter 77 campaign, which, against all odds, had eventually triumphed in 1989's Velvet Revolution.

Other members of the exiled opposition supported the idea and Kanan worked on the project in late spring and early summer. In August he came up with two single-spaced typed pages, which read as a sort of countertext to *Republic of Fear*, Paradiso to that book's Inferno: a new foundation, laid out across the ruins.

Kanan spelled out Iraq's need for a democratic system of government and for respect of the rights of minorities. 'It was a celebration,' Kanan said, 'of the reality of the individual for a society that had not known such a culture before.' His document called for the establishment of a parliamentary democracy and an independent judiciary, the banning of torture, a moratorium on capital punishment, and a drastic diminution in the role of the army and the security forces. It concluded with a coda, inviting signatures: 'By its existence this Charter is proof that the barrier of fear has been broken: never again will we Iraqis hang our heads in shame and let violence rule in our name,' Kanan affirmed. His father was the first to sign the document.

Mohamed was very aware of his country's history and was eager to see the experiences of ordinary Iraqis recorded. Yasmine Allawi, who worked in the gallery as an office assistant between 1987 and 1989, recalled visiting him after she left the job. 'This was during the invasion of Kuwait,' she told me in interview. 'I was telling him we left our houses. People were walking to Basra in the south of Iraq. Women were happy seeing their sons coming back alive from the Kuwait border. We all left our houses in Baghdad. When I was leaving my house I was looking at every room. I thought the house might be destroyed. I thought the pictures of the family would be important. The idea of who we are, the Iraqi ID, gold, money, small carpets. We left everything. We shared rooms with people in Karbala. Six or seven people were living in one room. Dr Maikya then told me to contact Kanan, tell him all these details because otherwise I would forget them. He told me, "It is very important to write it down with details and names, because when you grow older you will forget," he said.'

Mohamed was angry that the Americans did not support the Shi'i uprising in the south and the Kurdish uprising in the north in 1991. Despite the rhetoric of Western leaders who advocated the overthrow of Hussein's regime and the establishment of a democratic state, the multinational force did not intervene to support the southern Iraqi people in their attempt to overthrow the regime.

When the uprising failed, more than two million Kurdish people had no option but to flee to the mountains, where they fell victim to diarrhoea, acute respiratory infections and the trauma they had suffered. Up to 750 people were dying every day. The UN consensus, which included Arab nations, had not proposed breaking up Iraq as an independent state. Thus, even after victory had been achieved, Saddam Hussein remained in power.

Eventually a 'safe haven' for the Kurds was created in northern Iraq. In October 1991, when the Iraqi government withdrew all services from Iraqi Kurdistan, elections were held for a 105-member Kurdish National Assembly, establishing a de facto Kurdish state. But the people of the south, who had been just as brutally suppressed, received no such relief. One of the most oppressive regimes in history prevailed from August 1990 to February 2003.

Writing in the *Guardian* in September 1999, James Buchan said:

> Humiliated in war by the West, terrorised by their own government, reduced to paupers, unwelcome anywhere in the world, the Arabs of Iraq are falling to pieces. It is not simply that with their money and savings destroyed and their goods embargoed, their living standards have fallen to the level of at least 30 years ago. In their own eyes, as Iraqis and above all as Arabs, they have been reduced to nothing. I have never seen a people so demoralised. Everybody I met, even the most repellent Baathist thug and extortionist, felt himself a victim.

The lure of oil could not be resisted for long by Western industrialists and so-called neutral countries. Sanctions were loosened and

Saddam Hussein accumulated personal wealth, a well-equipped military force, and power. His presence loomed threateningly over the Middle East. In March 2003 the Americans and British declared their official reasons for removing him by force: eliminating his 'weapons of mass destruction'; reducing the threat of international terrorism; and promoting democracy in the region.

Mohamed fully supported the 2003 invasion of Iraq and told Iraqis in exile that they were no longer refugees but had to think of themselves as ambassadors for their country.

Subhi Azzawi recalled taking Mohamed from King's Cross, London, to Cambridge to attend the funeral of archaeologist Professor David Oates in 2004. 'He remonstrated with me in the train and admonished me for not supporting the invasion of 2003. He said, "You should worship the Americans for getting rid of Saddam Hussein." And I said: "I am sorry, I don't agree with you. They destroyed Iraq."'

Mohamed had come to terms with the fact that his vision of Baghdad as a flourishing Arab city – a modern oasis surrounded by palms – could never be realised with the Baath Party in power. Authoritarian regimes don't trust palm trees – they provide somewhere to talk, to plot – and in fact, in post-Gulf War Iraq, they were chopped down in the thousands. Mohamed did not welcome the suffering the bombs brought to his people but conceded that he would be happy even to see the destruction of the buildings he had once designed, as long as the regime fell. 'As a planner I accept the reality. I accept the horror,' he told *Guardian* correspondent Martin Bright in an interview published on 30 March 2003. 'But I just hope they have a strategy worked out to afterwards reconstruct the city on a human scale.' He went on to say that he had a dream after the fall of Saddam: 'First I would plant 25 million palm trees to recover the city and re-create its parks.' The shelves of Kufa Gallery were piled with sketches of his plans for Baghdad and Basra, but needless to say, no one from the British or US governments ever consulted him on the reconstruction of Iraq. 'I am a conductor without an orchestra,' he said ruefully.

Kanan, by the mid 1990s a respected Professor of Islamic and Middle Eastern Studies at Brandeis University in Massachusetts, was also pursued by the international media following the publication of *Republic of Fear*, and of his next best-seller, *Cruelty and Silence*. He became a champion of democracy and human rights in Iraq, and was seen as such by a large number of Iraqis in exile. Others considered him an American stooge who had sold his country to the new imperialists.

                    ❧❧

After 2003, Kanan set up the Iraq Memory Foundation (IMF) to document and preserve the experience of Iraqis during the three decades of Baathist control, in order to help the nation face up to its future by owning up to its past. The foundation followed in the footsteps of similar undertakings elsewhere in the world, such as the post-apartheid Truth and Reconciliation Commission in South Africa. The core of the foundation was a trail of documents left behind by the Baath party during the 1991 atrocities in Kurdistan and Kuwait and in the aftermath of the 2003 war. Oral history accounts were also recorded and broadcast, telling the stories of Iraqi victims who suffered from persecution at the hands of the Baathists. But whereas the South African experience of truth-telling had succeeded in the mid-1990s, the IMF's efforts did not meet with the support of the new Iraqi political elite, and its activities, mainly oral history recordings, began to dwindle and decline.

When it first started, the IMF needed a base in Baghdad for its new headquarters – and for that purpose Kanan succeeded in reclaiming, temporarily, the family home on the Tigris, which had been sequestrated by the Baathists in 1971. The old house had been altered to accommodate the pompous Baathist leadership, but the general architecture set in place by his father in the late 1960s remained the same. The building became the offices of the IMF, and in the first six years after 2003 it flourished to become a centre of arts and activities designed to connect Iraq's increasingly isolated communities with one another.

※

After the ousting of Saddam Hussein, the exiled Iraqi opposition were in for a big shock. The American military occupation of Iraq officially ended on 28 June 2004. But neither the removal of Saddam Hussein, nor the withdrawal of Western troops, provided the instant cure for the country's problems that many, including Mohamed, had hoped for. Destruction of society and of lives continued beyond Iraq's first multi-party elections in fifty years, held on 30 January 2005. The pervasive corruption, insurgency, unemployment and collapse of infrastructure seemed insoluble, while violent displacement of Sunnis from Shi'i areas and vice versa intensified in Baghdad.

Politics and violence aside, Kanan wanted his father to see Iraq before he died. With the assistance of his closest friend and colleague in Baghdad, Mustafa al-Kazimy, he succeeded in arranging a final visit for Mohamed to his beloved Baghdad. It happened in 2006 when Makiya was ninety-two years old.

'It was a very important journey for my father,' Kanan remembered, 'and I am so glad that we managed to make it happen before he was physically incapable of making it. He needed constant care in a variety of ways, but he managed the trip in the end and was filled with excitement about having been there. It meant an awful lot to him, and from that point of view it was a great success.'

Al-Kazimy accompanied Mohamed everywhere on the two-week visit. A journalist and activist who had first met Kanan in 1991 during the meetings around Charter 1991, he became director of the Oral History Project of the IMF and later a magazine editor. He knew everybody and was expert at negotiating the required maze of checkpoints and roadblocks. He will never forget the trip to Makiya's house, which had been expropriated by Saddam Hussein's regime in 1971.

Al-Kazimy spoke nostalgically about the trip. 'We flew to Amman, and then to Baghdad. The last time Makiya had seen Baghdad was in the 1980s. The city had changed completely. We arrived in Karadat Maryam in the Green Zone, where his house is located. One kilometre from his house, I asked him, "Do you know where you are?" He said, "This is Karadat Maryam." I asked him, "Where is your house?" He told me, "Go straight ahead, take a left and a right, and this is my house – but they changed it. They made it into a Baathist house. They destroyed the design. But this is my house."'

The house, on the Tigris River, is now the headquarters of the IMF. Mohamed had designed it as a house of light. 'In the morning, when the day starts, the light will bring hope. When the light comes you feel active, and you want to do something,' he told al-Kazimy. 'In the front room there is a big window. You can see the water. It is only two storeys high. If I make the house too high, the sky will not hug the sun. It will steal a part of the light and a part of the sky.' With his little camera, Mohamed photographed the sunset over and over again. He took the same photograph at different times of the day. Al-Kazimy drove Mohamed around Baghdad in the morning and, in the afternoon, Mohamed was very happy to come home and talk to the Foundation's staff.

Mohamed had first left Iraq in 1971 as a victim of Saddam Hussein's regime, but he returned a celebrity in 2006. Then-President Jalal Talabani hosted a dinner in his honour, and there were other dinners hosted by the Vice President, Adil Abdul-Mahdi, and the Minister of Finance, Bayan Jabr Solagh. He met the then-Prime Minister, Ibrahim al-Jaafari – a target of Kanan Makiya's later critique of the new Iraqi elite in his novel *The Rope*, published in 2016 – who even helped him get into the car at the end of their discussion. But the real highlight of the trip was the visit to the Department of Architecture at Baghdad University (see Chapter 8).

Kanan had not wanted his father to see the devastation of Baghdad. 'I was trying to make him happy,' he recalled. 'I did not want him to leave with sadness and bitterness in his heart.' Nonetheless al-Kazimy made sure Mohamed saw most of the city, and he remembers that he 'was shocked by the destruction, but he said that they need a good master plan and everything can be corrected. He also wanted to see a public transport system and not so many cars.'

It was difficult to tell who was happier with the visit, Mohamed or his son, who remarked: 'My father has an extraordinary ability to see what he wants to see and to imagine what might be once all this rubbish goes. It is how Baghdad is *supposed* to be that he is actually seeing. If he is walking through a city or travelling through it, he is constantly looking at it in terms of what it can be, and just obliterating from his memory the nastiness of what he actually does see, which to him is ephemeral. He is a Baghdadi first and foremost. The idea of Baghdad is almost more important to him than the idea of Iraq. He belongs to the city more than to the country as a whole, although he would be upset with me for saying this.'

When Mohamed returned to London he talked endlessly about his trip, especially about the young students who clustered around him. He was amazed at their enthusiasm and at the sentiments of other people he had met on the trip, and he never stopped making plans and creating designs for his beloved city and for other cities in Iraq.

ುಲ

Mohamed wanted to tell the world about his visit, and a lecture – 'Baghdad after Twenty-five Years' – was organised for 26 July 2006, in Kufa Gallery. Mohamed was elated to be able to recount his experiences to an attentive audience. But at the end of the lecture disaster struck: he fell and broke his hip, and never returned to the gallery again. His injury was now paramount, and the family could no longer finance the lifestyle that Makiya and Margaret were accustomed to, cover their medical expenses, *and* maintain the gallery. Margaret's depression was now a semi-permanent condition, and full-time carers were needed to look after the couple. News of the proposed closure of the gallery was circulated, and was greeted with dismay and shock by London's Iraqi community.

'We made huge efforts to get the Iraqi government to buy it,' Kanan recollected. 'The only person who expressed an interest was the then-President, Jalal Talabani, whom I also approached personally. But it is one thing for a top government official to say I want to do something and another for the money to be allocated and actually paid out in London. The Iraqi elite that had returned from exile may have had good ideas, but they had no capability to deliver on any of them. And I had to do everything personally – the Iraqi embassy in London was not interested even in interceding.

'Mustafa al-Kazimy had spoken to the then-Iraqi-ambassador to the United Kingdom, Dr Salah al-Shaikhly. We were asking for a whole going concern, the Kufa Gallery with its staff and cultural activities, to be handed over from the Makiya family, to be sponsored by the Iraqi government in the same way the Iraqi government's 1980s cultural centre in London, which closed in the late 1980s, had been sponsored. Kufa filled the centre's role from 1986 to 2006, but it was entirely privately funded, and the family simply no longer had the funds to go on doing it with the now added expense of providing full-time carers for Mohamed and Margaret.

'The Iraqi government never came through. We waited and waited for it, until I decided it was never going to happen. With my father's agreement, we sold the building to the Al Saqi bookshop, the enterprise I and Mai Ghoussoub had helped set up in the late 1970s,' Kanan recalled with sadness. After the building was finally sold, Kanan was vilified by the Iraqi community in London.

'I was very annoyed when the gallery closed,' Khalid al-Kashtini remarked. 'I became very cross with Kanan: it was Kanan who sold it. His father did not want to sell it. But Kanan got a bit disappointed with Iraq and the Iraqis. He urged the Americans to invade, and then he was disappointed when the Dawa Party – the religious people – took over. They didn't like him. He became bitter. When

Kanan went to Baghdad,' Kashtini believes, 'he thought he would be writing the constitution of the country, but that did not happen. Kanan more or less wanted to take his revenge on the Iraqis, and he sold the Kufa Gallery. It was not just for the sake of the money – he had something against the Iraqis. Kanan was no longer in touch with Iraq and the Iraqis. After the gallery was sold, Mohamed Makiya became depressed. He never recovered.'

'When Kufa Gallery closed, a window of my soul also closed,' lamented Hussein al-Sikafi, the photographer who took pictures of most of the events at the gallery. 'I used to see something bright, but now I see something so dark. For many months I could not go to the area and look at the door and the building. It was a very nice period of my life in the Kufa Gallery.'

One of the most moving, heartfelt tributes to Mohamed and the gallery came from Dr Abdul Rahim Hassan, his dear friend of nearly thirty years: 'For twenty years, Makiya kept the Kufa Gallery above any clash of loyalties due to religion, race, personal taste, etc. It provided a platform for lecturers, poets, musicians, and artists. Wednesday evenings, for two decades, were always a special event. Al-Kufa was not only a house for culture, a unique institution, but a home for Iraqi, Arab and many other intellectuals. It had an international outlook and aimed to bridge the culture divide between East and West.

'Since its closure in the summer of 2006, London has lost one of its vibrant cultural centres, and Iraqi intellectuals in particular have struggled to find a meeting place. They are nowadays to be found in coffee-shops. My friend the sociologist Dr Ibrahim al-Haidari summed it up nicely: "There was only one Kufa Gallery, and there was only one Dr Makiya." This says a lot for the place, and for the person who had the vision and turned the dream into reality.'

CHAPTER 14

Makiya's Legacy

'The Makiya name is a legacy in itself.'

Mohamed Makiya spent the last years of his life in his flat in central London, surrounded by his massive collection of books, artworks and antiquities. His memories of an Iraq long gone never left him. He continued deriving inspiration from its past and dreaming of an Iraq that would reflect the country's 'golden age', as he called it, of the 1950s. He told Maysoon Wahbi, a former student at the School of Architecture at Baghdad University, that he wanted someone to write a history of this period. Much younger friends of his son, as well as admirers from the Kufa days, continued to visit him. He longed to relaunch the Kufa Gallery in his home, but his family was not supportive, and this dream remained just that. And for Mohamed, without the Kufa Gallery, the world seemed drained of hope and colour. He was surrounded by people, but an incredible loneliness overcame him. It was a dark time, full of grief, challenges and ill health.

The flat was like a museum filled with antiquarian books and works of art. The painting dearest to Makiya's heart was *Vagabond Family*, by Shakir Hassan al-Said. He fondly remembered how he had bought it in 1961 for 80 dinars, which he paid al-Said in eight instalments of ten dinars a month.

There was also one of Jewad Salim's plaster reliefs, which had been abandoned in Iraq when he was forced to leave his house in al-Mansour, and had been lost since 1971. After months of searching, Kanan finally succeeded in finding it in a former factory owned by one of his cousins, damaged and in need of years of restoration. He brought it to London in 2009, where experts formerly with the Victoria and Albert Museum worked to restore it.

In notebooks, on random scraps of paper, on a napkin or a tablecloth, Mohamed continued to jot down his schemes and sketches for a future Iraq. He reconceived the entire city, concocting new plans for whole neighbourhoods, contriving new conceptions of the relation of courtyard to home, home to neighbourhood, and neighbourhood to township; of river to city; of walkers to roadways. 'A Thousand and One Images of Baghdad' he titled a would-be manuscript that never saw the light of day: visions that, night after night, kept him up.

Mahdi Ali, Makiya's live-in carer for four years, described to me how Mohamed was always sketching. However, 'In the last years of his life he could not make sketches because his hands were shaking, so he started to take photos from the TV. I had to teach him how to take these photos.' There were a number of projects close to Mohamed Makiya's heart. Mahdi, who also worked part time for Al Saqi bookshop at 26 Westbourne Grove in West London, was busy scanning material for Mohamed to have access to while he was lying in his bed at home. In Mahdi's description, 'He was a perfectionist: "Do the job more than once, and always try to do better. Do it again and it will be perfect." I was warned that he was a hard man, but he treated me like his son. He told Kanan, "I don't mind if you are not here – Mahdi is here. When you travel, take your time." And Kanan trusted me totally.'

Mohamed regularly spoke and met with Dia Kashi and Mustafa al-Kazimy, two of Kanan's best friends who had promised Kanan they would always try to be there when he was not. They visited regularly, and talked with Mohamed about the reinstatement of the Majlis al-Ia'mar, an independent extension of the Iraqi government during the time of the monarchy, which by law took 70 per cent of Iraq's oil income out of government control and invested it in building the country: Mohamed dreamed of re-establishing such an institution in post-2003 Iraq. He also wanted to get photos of old houses in villages in Iraq that he had visited fifty years ago. He told Dia Kashi that it was a crime that the Iraqi people 'don't take care of these villages any more'. Mahdi Ali recalled: 'Mohamed was watching the news every day. He kept saying: "Is this true? Is this happening? Are Iraqis actually killing each other?"' He could not believe what was going on.'

But the Baghdad Makiya knew and loved was disappearing, and it seemed that the violence of the 2003 war had never stopped, including during Mohamed's last year. His face became thin and sharp, and his eyes were profoundly sad and disappointed as he aged in tandem with the disintegration of a city and country he loved.

Post-Saddam, Iraq went from crisis to crisis. The alienation of the Sunnis by the Shi'i-dominated governments prompted support for ISIS led by Abu Bakr al-Baghdadi, who commanded between 7,000 and 12,000 fighters, 3,000 of whom were foreigners. After achieving some military success in Syria the group began its expansion into Sunni areas of north and west Iraq in 2014. In January 2014 it took control of Fallujah and then advanced into other Sunni towns, including parts of Ramadi and Tikrit. In June it sent shock waves across the world when it captured Mosul.

The rise of ISIS further split Iraqi society. Grand Ayatollah Ali al-Sistani, the Shi'i world's top *marja* (source of authority), responded to the Sunni jihadist movement with a fatwa calling Iraqis to take up to arms. Tens of thousands of men, mostly Shi'i, joined new and old militias, many supported by Iran. ISIS captured Mosul, Iraq's third largest city in June 2014. It unleashed its reign of terror in the city and in other towns it occupied it Iraq, including Tel Afar.

ಞ

As well as watching the decline of his homeland, Mohamed was also witnessing the decline of his wife, who died in 2012 at the age of ninety-four. In the last years of her life, Margaret was plagued by ill health and depression. Speaking to her grandson, Naseem, in an interview which he recorded in 2004, she said: 'I am happy to have missed some of the final phases of the revolutionary activity in Iraq. I am not sorry to have missed the American invasion and its aftermath. You feel sorry to see the country plunged into such chaos and such darkness, which one would never have thought possible.'

Margaret was a strong and proud woman. When rheumatoid arthritis prevented her from walking without the aid of a frame, she continued to dismiss questions about her health. 'She wanted people to be happy when they came to see her. She did not want to talk about what she was suffering from,' her niece Amal recalled. 'In the years before she died, she would sleep in one flat and uncle [that is, Mohamed] would sleep in another. They spent the day together.'

Mohamed moved into Kanan's flat at 109 Bedford Court, where Mahdi, his carer, slept in the room next to him. He spent his days with Margaret in 107 Bedford Court. After Makiya's fall in 2006, Indre, a carer and housekeeper who had been employed only on weekends, started working five days a week. Margaret was finding it difficult to cope with the housework and cooking. Mohamed insisted on Iraqi home-cooked food, especially *bamia* (ladies' fingers), and expected to be waited on hand and foot. Friends such as Attared Sarraf, the older sister of Kanan's wife, Wallada, and Dia Kashi's sister, along with many other London-based Iraqi friends of Kanan and Wallada, regularly brought him his favourite Iraqi dishes.

In his last years of life Makiya's faithful friends, students and former employees continued to call on him, among them Garry Martin. 'I visited him just before his passing in London. He knew me instantly, and we reminisced about our days together. We were very happy to see each other.' Mohamed was especially fond of children, who affectionately referred to him as 'Jiddoo' (grandfather). He made many recordings of his memoirs and his views on architecture, which he asked Rashid Khayoun's wife, Liqaa', to transcribe. He also asked Yasmine Allawi to help with transcription, but this did not happen. 'They were like his diary – full of information. I am sorry I did not transcribe them,' Allawi recalled. Diddi Malek and Kanan took Mohamed in a wheelchair to the restaurant in Hyde Park designed by Zaha Hadid.

However fragile his health, Mohamed stayed cheerful when being visited. 'I went to visit him a lot when he was frail,' Attared Sarraf remembered. 'We took him out. He would insist on paying, because he was the oldest. He loved to go to Café Rouge and sit and watch people. He celebrated his 101st birthday in the Café Rouge with a glass of wine in 2015. His daughter once brought him to Westfield [a large shopping complex in West London], and we went to Mandaloun, a Lebanese restaurant. It was like being in a souk. Everybody was going past, and he enjoyed just watching people.'

A small support group of Kanan's friends rallied round and helped Kanan look after his parents. 'They were my friends, they respected my work on Iraq, and they were always there for us,' Kanan stressed, paying special tribute to Dia Kashi and Mustafa al-Kazimy. After Margaret died, Kanan took leave from his teaching at Brandeis University to look after his ailing father. During the subsequent three years in London he finished writing *The Rope*, a haunting account about Iraqi failure in the wake of the 2003 war.

෴

Mohamed was anxious that the younger generation should stay in touch with their culture and traditions. He was very proud of the achievements of his children and grandchildren and wanted to share his family's heirlooms with his grandchildren, as is evident from the gift he gave to his granddaughter Bushra, a silver box inscribed with a sketch by the great Iraqi artist Jewad Salim.

Speaking of his grandfather, Naseem Makiya, Kanan's son, said affectionately: 'My grandfather definitely did not fit the classic stereotype of a grumpy old man. He was a joy to be around. He was constantly happy and excited to hear our news and hear how things were going with us personally. He was so proud of us and would exaggerate anything positive we were doing into a spectacle of brilliance. He was easily amused and would laugh at all our jokes – even when we weren't joking.

'He loved to talk about architecture. His dedication to the profession and his passion were so evident. He had strong opinions when it came to city design and absolutely hated cars. Transporting only individuals, he used to say, was such inefficient city design – and all the roads that had to be built to support them! What a waste!

'Visiting the Cotswolds while growing up, I mainly remember our Christmas traditions. Jiddoo [grandfather] would sit in his big comfy chair, which only he was allowed to sit in – although sometimes I would jump in it when he wasn't looking and then I immediately got down when he came into the room, and he would notice and laugh. We would sit around the fire opening presents and watching classic Christmas movies. He would always give at least one design-related gift, to try and encourage his grandchildren to become architects.

'Then he would try to light his pipe with matches, and we would climb on top of him and blow the matches out, because we knew smoking was bad for him. He quit eventually. He was a pleasure to be around, and such an amazing role model.'

∽·∾

Kanan spent years convincing his father to send his architectural archive to MIT, the leading academic institution in archiving Islamic architecture. Once he agreed, the Aga Khan Documentation Center (AKDC) acquired Makiya's complete architectural archive, documenting his prodigious career.* (It was the first architectural archive

---

* Situated within the MIT Libraries, the AKDC at MIT and Harvard was established in 1979 by a gift from His Highness the Aga Khan. The Center supports teaching of, and research on, the history and theory of architecture, urbanism, environmental and landscape design, visual culture and conservation, as well as on the practice of architecture in Muslim societies.

Ahmed Naji presenting Mohamed Makikya at the inauguration of a commemorative exhibition of Shakir Hassan at Salam House, the Humanitarian Dialogue Foundation, London, 4 March 2011 (Pic: Ahmed Naji, *Under the Palm Trees*)

received by the AKDC.) It contains materials ranging from personal correspondence, project notes and hand-drawn design sketches to formal proposals, final drawings, and photographs for projects built and unbuilt, extant or not. Archnet is gradually making the entire architectural achievement of Makiya available in an open-access online format for researchers around the world.[1]

Kanan spent a year getting the material ready for shipment to the US. 'I did all the locating, sorting and classifying of the material. Mahdi was assisting me to pack sixty odd boxes plus thousands of drawings that I eventually sent to the United States in the summer of 2012. And I had to overcome my father's initial reluctance: he wanted everything to go to Iraq, to his old School of Architecture. That would have been the natural home in normal circumstances. But Baghdad was not normal. He finally relented when a good artist friend of his living in Baghdad wrote to him at my request explaining why the material would not be safe in Baghdad.'

In June 2013, an exhibition of Makiya's Khulafa Mosque projects was held in the Rotch Library at MIT. It included twenty-five images of sketches, design notes, plans and photographs reproduced from the originals in the archive. Commenting on the archive, Dr Sharon Smith, the Program Head at the AKDC, told me: 'It really is a treasure and very special to me, as it was our first venture into becoming a centre for primary research.'

Mohamed was very happy that the Humanitarian Dialogue Foundation (Salam House) produced a London exhibition, curated by Ahmed Naji al-Said, to commemorate Shakir Hassan al-Said, one of his favourite artists. In March 2011, Mohamed inaugurated the event, stressing that al-Said was the first artist to seriously investigate the role of Arabic letters from an artistic perspective. Several of al-Said's paintings from Makiya's collection were displayed at the exhibition.

Mohamed was eager for Salam House to stage another exhibition, '1,001 Pictures of Baghdad'. 'He was going through his archive,' Ahmed Naji al-Said remembered. 'He wanted to send a message to everyone out there in Iraq, to architects, to the Iraqi government, that Baghdad needs to be rebuilt and regenerated as a centre of civilisation – a new Iraq! This idea followed from his vision for re-designing the centre of Baghdad in the 1980s. The exhibition never happened – there was too much work to be done, and it would have needed at least four full-time employees. We tried to get support from the Iraqi government, but nothing happened.'

At Kanan's request, al-Said catalogued more than 200 artworks from Makiya's private collection. This project led to al-Said's writing *Under the Palm Trees: Modern Iraqi Art with Mohamed Makiya and Jewad Selim*. The book was published in 2019.

'I used to go and see Makiya every other Sunday, and we would have a chat as I was doing my research,' al-Said recalled. 'I only showed him the draft once I finished the work. He was always unhappy about work that was going on because he thought that it was imperfect. But he was very happy with it, and even in the hospital, when I saw him four days before he passed away, he held my hand and said to me it is not acceptable that I only focus on my personal life as a dentist and forget what Iraq means to me, especially as I have an ability to do something for the country through writing or promoting art, as I did through the art book. Art is a passion of mine, but at the same time you have to pay bills!'

༺༻

Recognition of Mohamed's achievements in a life dedicated to architecture increased as he got older. In 2003, he was given the title Dean of Arab Engineering Design at an international investment conference in Dubai; in 2008, the al-Kindi Society for Engineers organised an event in recognition of Mohamed's contributions to architecture; and on his 100th birthday, in 2014, the Iraqi Ministry of Culture organised and endorsed Mohamed's centenary as one of the main events in a large-scale festival titled 'Baghdad: The Capital of Culture'.

Mohamed's life was also documented in *Reflections on the Years: Biography of an Architect and the Diary of a Baghdadi Neighbourhood* by Rashid al-Khayoun, which Saqi Books published in 2015. Mohamed dictated to al-Khayoun memories of his life up until the setting up of the Department of Architecture at Baghdad University in 1959.

Mohamed definitely wanted his memories and philosophy to be recorded, and he proposed dictating a book to Subhi al-Azzawi. 'I asked if I was entitled to express any opinions,' al-Azzawi told me, 'and he shouted, "No! – Just write what I say." I said, 'I can't do that. I am a highly qualified architect, not a secretary. I felt it was an insult. If I had wanted to, I could have written a book about him in my own way. But Makiya is a very dominating personality. I don't think he would have let anyone write a book about him without him having a tremendous influence on it.'

A centenary conference on Makiya's 100th birthday was the brainchild of Khalid al-Sultani, author of *Mohammad Makiya: A Century of Architecture and Life*. It was organised by the Makiya Committee with the support of Baghdad Municipality and the Department of Architecture in Baghdad University which Makiya set up in 1959. 'Nowadays people in Baghdad are focused on survival and fighting the terrorists,' al-Sultani explained. 'Through this special event we wanted to show that we are against the terrorists who want to turn our country into a desert without culture.'

In a moving tribute to Makiya at the conference, Akram Ogaily urged conference participants to 'transform this occasion to act towards a new, serious responsible approach to serve Iraq.' Ogaily recalled Makiya's words from 1963, almost half a century ago: 'Architecture is a profession which requires a major effort and sincerity and a commitment to its human and moral considerations.'

About 120 people, architects, academics and government officials attended the conference. 'It was difficult for famous Iraqi architects living abroad to come – travelling to Baghdad was difficult,' Ogaily explained. The overseas visitors included the renowned architect Qahtan al-Madfai. The highlight was a visit to the Khulafa Mosque and other buildings which Makiya designed. The mosque is still standing but Old Baghdad is no more. 'It is so sad,' Ali Mousawi, another student of Makiya's, lamented. 'The shanasheel windows enclosed with carved wood latticework and often lined with stained glass have been sold as antiques by corrupt officials to people from the Gulf. The new mayor, Dr Dhikra Al-wash, is like a beautiful fish trying to swim in a sea of sharks. She can't deal with those sharks.'

As well as reminiscing about the past, conference participants looked to the future. A street in the heart of Baghdad would be renamed Mohamed Makiya Street; it was decided a commemorative stamp bearing Makiya's portrait would be issued by the Ministry of Transport and an old nineteenth-century house in Haifa Street, which runs through central Baghdad along the west bank of the

Commemorative stamp showing Mohamed Makiya

snaking Tigris River, would be used for a heritage centre named after Makiya.

☙❧

In June 2014, after he turned 100, Makiya received the inaugural Tamayouz Lifetime Achievement Award: Iraq's most prestigious architecture prize, which aims to celebrate the pioneers of Iraqi architecture. It recognised the impact of his celebrated and lasting contribution to Iraqi architecture, the establishment of the School of Architecture in Baghdad University, and his mentoring of generations of aspiring Iraqi architects. He was not able to attend the award ceremony in Amman and received the prize in his London flat, recording a short word of gratitude to the organisers.

Speaking softly with dignity and a muted pride he said: 'Thank you very much. I feel very grateful and proud on this occasion. Many thanks. I would like to express my gratitude, appreciation and pride to receive the Tamayouz Lifetime Achievement Award. It is the first of its kind and I hope the Tamayouz Organisation will play a vital role in future on the cultural and architectural fronts.'

The following year the Mohamed Makiya Prize was announced, the newest prize to be established as part of the Tamayouz Excellence Award's programme of championing and celebrating the best of Iraqi architecture. Every year the prize will be presented to the architectural personality of the year, which will be the individual or organisation that has made the greatest contribution to the advancement of Iraqi architecture in the past year. The first winner was Rifat Chadirji; the second Dr Khalid al-Sultani.

In June 2015, just over a month before Mohamed died, Dr Abdul Rahim Hassan visited him at his home, along with the lawyer Ali al-Sajjad and the sociologist Dr Ibrahim al-Haidari. He told me: 'He was in high spirits. All he talked about was Iraq and its cities, particularly Baghdad. The one thing he kept mentioning is that the different cities of Iraq should develop their specific character, one that is reflected in city planning and architecture. He was full of ideas and thoughts that he wanted to share with us so that we would carry on the task of regenerating Iraq. His carer, Mahdi, told me that Mohamed kept remembering verses from the Qur'an that his uncle made him learn by heart when he was a young adolescent. In my presence, he recited verses from the *ar-Rahman* chapter of the Qur'an.

'However, a couple of days later he was admitted to University College London Hospital, where I visited him with Mr al-Sajjad for the last time. He kept asking us about what we have done and what we are going to do. He had on the wall in front of his hospital bed a collage of different generations of teachers and graduates from the Department of Architecture which he founded in Baghdad. Students in Baghdad had made it for him when they heard he was in hospital. His mind was sound, and he gave the impression that he might be with us for a while. The end was sooner than I expected, however, and there was nothing anyone could have done to keep him alive.'

Kanan and Mustafa al-Kazimy were with Mohamed on 19 July 2015 when he closed his eyes for the last time. 'Till the last minute he spoke about life,' al-Kazimy said, with tears in his eyes. 'How important it was, how people must, believe in love and tolerance and that they are part of the universe. He was smiling. He spoke about his dreams for Baghdad: to develop it to combine the old and the new.'

Kanan and Mustafa were designated in Mohamed Makiya's will to ensure compliance with his wishes for a traditional Shi'i funeral. Afterwards, Mohamed's body was taken to its final resting place in St Pancras and Islington Cemetery in East Finchley. The family chose the new Woodland Burial Area near to the main entrance, where Margaret was also buried: a vista of mature trees and natural grassland, through which a path meanders.

When he discussed his burial arrangements in 2013 (after his wife was buried in the woodland area, Makiya said he wanted to be buried next to his mother in Najaf, but this proved impossible). 'We had that discussion after my mother was buried,' Kanan recalled. 'His mother was buried in 1958. He had been there. He was very close to his mother; he never knew his father. The problem was that, after the uprising of 1991, Najaf was in total upheaval, and major parts of the city were destroyed in the crackdown that happened after the uprising. I told my father I had no idea where his mother was buried, and the precise location was going to be impossible to find. My cousins had been to the cemetery in Najaf trying to find her grave but failed. So I was able to persuade him to change his mind and be buried with my mother, which both my sister, Hind, and I wanted. We can take care of the grave over time, and his grandchildren can visit it.'

The final funeral rite was a wake (*fathia*) in the Radisson Blu Portman Hotel in the heart of London, held on 26 July, four days after the funeral. Everybody who was anybody in London's Iraqi community showed up. Many of the mourners did not know Kanan or the family personally; they just wanted to come and pay their respects to Mohamed Makiya.

'Some old men came to Kanan, hugged him and started crying loudly,' remembered Dia Kashi. 'Men in our culture normally don't show emotion. It was as if they had lost a very close member of the family. That is how many Iraqis saw Makiya. Not many middle-class or rich Iraqis gave money from their own pockets to advance Iraqi culture and to represent Iraq in London and Britain the way Makiya did.'

Kashi and two other colleagues from the Kufa Gallery took care of the formalities at the *fathia*, escorting mourners to their seats and sitting with them while they read the opening verse of the Qur'an.

'Everything is over now. No more exile,' said Dr Abdul Rahim Hassan. 'A corner in a foreign field that is forever Iraq,' Hassan said, referencing a poem by Rupert Brooke. He then quoted from a poem by the famous Iraqi poet Badr Shakir al-Sayyab, convinced that it expressed Mohamed's sentiments.

Farewell my friends, my beloved ones.
If you wish to remember me,
Remember me on a moonlit night.
Otherwise it will be just a name,
Disappeared among other names.
Farewell my friends,
Farewell, my beloved.

Postscript

Makiya received the greatest recognition and acclaim in the last years of his life, and became more famous after he died than he was while he was alive. Why? His son, Kanan, has an explanation.

After 2003, the Iraqi Shi'i elite dominated the government for the first time in its history. One can't help but notice, however, the increasing evidence of the failure of this new dominant elite to deliver the new Iraq that they had promised while in the opposition, or that the Americans had promised when they invaded Iraq. There was an actual fragmentation of the country, with rabid organisations like ISIS taking whole chunks of the country and occupying its second largest city.

'My father's name emerged as that of an important cultural figure,' says Kanan, 'one who quite literally loved his city, Baghdad, just as Baghdad was beginning to fall apart; concrete barriers were going up everywhere, bombs were going off. The city that is Baghdad today is slipping into a kind of fragmented and splintered world he would not have recognised. Baghdad, after ISIS, is not one city. It is many cities, with communities fighting each other and building barriers against each other, as they did during the 2005 to 2006 civil war. As the city loses that which gave it character, it acclaims the man who represented an entirely different, now lost, city.'

Books started appearing about Makiya shortly before his death. 'In just the last five years, five books have come out, all devoted to my father.' Kanan affirms. 'There is an increasing public utilisation of his image – one could even say its exploitation. Attention is being paid to him on many levels other than pure architecture. That is not to criticise such books; in many ways they are long overdue. It is simply to point out that something was going on in the culture, driven by the watershed moment that Baghdad found itself in after 2003.'

After Mohamed's death, his family was bombarded by people who wanted to elevate themselves in the Iraqi political landscape by invoking his name. Kanan found it all very distasteful: 'On the 2006 visit to Iraq, my father met the then-President, Jalal Talabani, the Prime Minister, and many government people. They would invite him, and they would receive him. They were supposedly celebrating his achievement historically as an architect, but they invariably turned it into something else. I was forced at the time of the funeral, the hardest time of all, to do something about this and to deal with people like that.'

Kanan even had to set up a small committee which wrote to government departments in Iraq, pointing out that, in his will, Makiya had authorised only three people to speak in the name of the family and discuss his architecture: Kanan, Akram Ogaily and Moustafa al-Kazimy.

Forty days after Mohamed's death, the entire faculty and administrative staff at the School of Architecture at Baghdad University held a traditional Shi'i remembrance ceremony. In London, on Wednesday 26 August 2015, the Humanitarian Dialogue Foundation (Salam House) held a memorial evening, with speeches, tributes, a short documentary film and photographs.

༄༅

Today, Baghdad is, sadly, a city Mohamed Makiya would feel has lost its soul. Many of the hideous concrete barriers and blast walls that replaced palm-lined streets are being removed, but peace is still a long way off, as the city is riven with prejudice and religious intolerance. In its heyday, from the 1940s through to the 1960s, Rashid Street was the place to be for well-off citizens, who flocked to the musicals in hotel nightclubs, sometimes travelling in double-decker buses imported from Britain. But those days are now a faded memory. Hardly a week goes by without an explosion, which adds to the mounting blood-stained rubble and to the death toll, not just in the capital but throughout the country. In 2018, 3,319 civilians lost their lives. Up to October 2019 the figure was 1542.[1] There were major protests throughout the country in October and November as the people demanded better services and an end to government corruption. Around 30,000 people demonstrated in Baghdad. At the beginning of October 104 protesters were killed and 6,000 injured by government forces who fired at them.

The heart of the Baghdad that was once a thriving metropolis is a dead zone. The city centre known as the international zone (previously the Green Zone set up by the Americans when they occupied Baghdad after ousting Saddam Hussein in the 2003 war) was separated by concrete blast walls from the rest of the city. From there, in the words of artist Rashad Salim, 'a new them looks down on the same old us'. The zone finally opened to the public after sixteen years on 4 June 2019.

In today's Baghdad, corruption is rampant. Some pavements are replaced every year, as greedy contractors bribe politicians for contracts to renew streets whether they need it or not. Building regulations belong to another era; there are no more rules. Anyone with money can build whatever he wants to, and there is no shortage of gaudy structures evincing an ostentatious display of wealth and – by throwing metal and concrete together – a desire to be modern. These ghastly creations rise up from the debris of the ruined city like hideous monsters.

Ali Mousawi, a former student of Mohamed Makiya, looks out of the window in his office in Fulham High Street. He has seen many transformations in this West London suburb, with its eighteenth-century buildings and historic pubs, light years away from the troubled Baghdad he recently left. Next to him are clay and bronze sculptures inspired by Mesopotamian images from Iraq's ancient civilisations: unique works of art created by his wife, Maysaloun Faraj. He shakes his head. There is pain in his voice and sorrow in his eyes as he strikes the table with the side of his hand and says: 'Baghdad is gone. It's all crap now. If you walk in Baghdad you feel so sad from inside, you feel it is not your city. It has become another city. The citizen himself is not respected – there is no pavement to walk on.'

Despite his snow-white hair, Mousawi's engaging smile and infectious laugh keep him forever young and hoping for a better tomorrow, although he is convinced life is getting worse for the people of Baghdad. 'Those people in government, in power, are getting more and more vicious, because they have money and they can buy others. They have put their hands on a treasure – a city with a heritage going back over a thousand years – and they are destroying it. Once we had one Saddam; now we have hundreds of Saddams, who are building their own financial empires. And who is suffering? The poor people! In the last thirteen years, $150 billion was spent on electrical power, and yet it is still in short supply. This is not just sad and painful. It is pathetic.'

Mousawi, founder of AMBS Architects, has been involved in the rebuilding of Baghdad since 2003. But many of his projects, including the National Library, remain on paper – because, as he says, 'the people in power could not get any benefit from them'. He dreams of following in the footsteps of Makiya, his mentor, who respected and loved the country's heritage – a master of incorporating traditional styles into modern architecture.

༺༻

Meanwhile, in the heart of London, Makiya's son Kanan has finished sorting out his father's estate. Mohamed Makiya died on 19 July 2015, at the age of 101. His flat, a Victorian 1890s building – No. 107 in Bedford Court Mansions – has been rented out by the family after renovations. His antiquarian book collection of around 3,000 volumes was sold by Sotheby's in April 2016.

In January 2016, winter, with its nippy frost and ice-cold wind, set in after a very mild autumn. The leaves were still on the ground, forming a carpet of yellow and orange. Kanan, author of the bestseller *Republic of Fear* documenting the atrocities of Saddam's regime, had just finished another book, a novel called *The Rope*. The soft-spoken, middle-aged Professor of Islamic and Middle Eastern Studies at Brandeis University flew in from Massachusetts to his London residence: flat No. 109, purchased in 2001 in the same palatial block to be near where his parents lived, just around the corner from the British Museum, with its famous Mesopotamia Gallery and Assyrian reliefs.

The Rope is a gritty, unflinching, haunting account about Iraqi failure in the wake of the 2003 war. In a personal note at the end of the novel, Kanan says: 'The realisation in late 2004 that Iraq was sliding towards civil war was a turning point in my life. The whole edifice of hopes that had clung to that slim possibility of a different kind of transition from dictatorship crumbled. Self-doubt began to eat away at the optimism that had sustained me since 1991.'[2] He believes that one evil, worse than the first, had quickly replaced another (Saddam Hussein's regime), and that the cycle of civil wars, revenge killings and destruction is not over yet. 'The terrible thing, of course, is that egregious abuse did not end in 2003: it began all over again, as victims turned into victimizers, and vice versa. Could it have been otherwise? I believe so.'[3]

Kanan does not believe that the situation in Baghdad or Iraq will improve in the near future. 'Not for one or two generations – ten to twenty years at least.'

ཚ⸺ཚ

After the centenary conference for Mohamed Makiya held in Baghdad in 2014, the Makiya Consultancy Committee for Baghdad's Development was officially registered in Baghdad as an NGO by former students of Makiya to advise the Municipality of Baghdad. A lease for the Makiya Heritage Centre on Haifa Street is in the name of this committee, which has started advising on the development of Baghdad. In response to his father's wish that 'Kufa Gallery should be returned to its natural place,' Kanan is working

The Sotheby's catalogue for the auction of the library of Mohamed and Margaret Makiya.

on transferring at least some of the gallery's archives to the Heritage Centre. The consultancy committee is also trying to make sure that Mohamed Makiya's dream of awarding annual prizes to three students of architecture comes true.

Makiya's plans for the Baghdad State Mosque and the Tikrit Parade Grounds still exist. His vision that they may be built one day may come true one day. Hope always sprang eternal in his breast.

֎

The Kufa Makiya Trust and Charity, meanwhile, has started work. One of the charity's first major tasks was the Sotheby's sale of the library of Mohamed and Margaret Makiya donated to that charity in their wills. According to the colourful catalogue which accompanied the sale, the library is a testament to Mohamed and Margaret's shared passion for books and other works on paper.

Kanan had done his best to gift the library to an institution in Iraq but, just as with getting the Iraqi government to take over the running of the Kufa Gallery, it proved to be a 'mission impossible'. Instead the proceeds of the sale are today funding many small projects about and inside Iraq. He responded to the criticism from Iraqis after the auction with dignity and good grace. 'There is not a single one of these books that was bought inside Iraq. They were bought here in the UK, or in some European bookshops. Who knew the books? Who understood the travel books? My mother. Not my father. My mother advised him on which books to get and what they were worth. That became their joint hobby, one that started with her meagre salary sixty years ago. She was the brains behind the whole collection.

'The art collection they built up together tells the story of modern art in Iraq. I have saved ten or twelve of the most important works that will one day go back to Iraq when there is a decent government that is capable of taking care of them.'

Diddi Malek, who helped to organise the auction at Sotheby's, agrees with Kanan about this. 'The money from the sale is going to be wisely used by the Kufa Makiya Charity. Dr Makiya would have been tickled pink if he had been alive. The sale of the books will promote Iraqi culture and heritage.'

Makiya is remembered for the unique buildings he designed: the Khulafa Mosque, the Kuwait State Mosque, the Sultan Qaboos Mosque in Oman, and numerous other buildings and houses in Iraq and the Gulf which stand as a testament to his work. He lives in the hearts of thousands of students whom he inspired, and in the memories of Middle Eastern artists whose work he bought, promoted and loved. Architects remember him as a master who breathed new life into Islamic architecture by integrating its rich heritage with the best of modern culture and technology.

Many Iraqis in London look back with nostalgia to the days of the Kufa Gallery in the 1990s. As one of Iraq's leading archaeologists, Lamia Gailani, told me before her recent demise: 'If you ask me what are my memories of Dr Makiya, Kufa Gallery will be the answer. He established a fantastic cultural centre for the Iraqis in the 1980s, and particularly in the 1990s. I know it was Dr Makiya's intention to have a place for Iraqis, an apolitical place where Iraqi and Arab culture was displayed.'

Dia Kashi is convinced that there should be a statue in every city where Makiya made a difference. 'When we lost him, we lost a huge chunk of our history and our country. He represented a lot, a big hope for people who are longing for a better Iraq. When we lost him, we lost that hope. He was the force behind a lot of ideas. He sacrificed his time and his wealth for the love of Iraq.'

Ahmed Naji al-Said emphasised that Makiya taught us how to look at the future in the light of one's history. Makiya's way of looking at history is that he would always find a common theme from that history which would unite people and rally them together and make them feel unique and inclusive of others at the same time. 'Islamic art includes the art of Turkey, as well as art from Persia and the Far East,' al-Said said to me. 'All of that comes under the umbrella of Islamic art. He would amalgamate these things and also look at the uniqueness of the art from a certain area.'

In the words of Garry Martin, Mohamed Makiya's work is a lasting legacy for young Iraqi architects, and indeed for all architects who aspire to design modern buildings in traditional societies where there is evidence of strong architectural and decorative traditions. 'I remember we always began a project in Baghdad,' Martin recalled, 'by drawing an elevation of the city viewed from the banks of the Tigris, which emphasised the traditional scale of the city and the nature of its texture. When you inserted your design into this panorama, it was immediately obvious whether the design was appropriate or not. Many modern architects would benefit from that approach.'

Zina Allawi described Makiya as a pioneer who brought Islamic architecture into the modern world and into the future. 'He said he took what he could from historical buildings. He called the traditional architectural forms he took from historical buildings *khurda* [little coins]. You put these little coins together into a modern picture.'

Makiya remained optimistic until the end of his life. His flame burned at a bright, steady level for a century. The Iraqis can search among Makiya's hopes and look at the way he lived his life as they search for a way forward. Makiya's archive at MIT will ensure that scholarly reflection on his work will continue. PhD students are contributing to his critical legacy as one who gave form to Middle Eastern architecture.

Makiya was proud to be a Shi'i, an Iraqi and an Arab. His philosophy can be summed up in his own words: 'Traditional continuity should not mean living in the past. It should be a question of the past living in the present, for a better future.'[4]

These simple yet profound words are a torch that lights the way forward out of the dark tunnel in which the Iraqi people have often found themselves.

APPENDICES

APPENDIX I

ABSTRACT OF MAKIYA'S PHD THESIS

Architecture and the Mediterranean Climate

STUDIES ON THE EFFECT of climatic conditions on Architectural Development in the Mediterranean Region with special reference to the Prospects of its Practice in the 'Near East'.

Dissatisfaction with present architectural development in the Near East in particular has prompted this attempt to discuss architecture and the Mediterranean climate in order to understand and define a more relevant architectural attitude. European practice influenced by different climatic conditions produces fascinating lineal compositions on paper, but less intrinsic design in its harmony with the southern environment.

If architecture is to be an art exercising a positive influence towards the good, then an attempt must be made to discuss its relevance to ethical values of society, traditional values of time and the cultural values of space; these three considerations make up the fundamental basis of its comprehensive scholarly understanding needed in face of present chaotic mannerisms.

The relation of Mediterranean civilisation and culture to climate is the scope of the second part; climate has hardly changed throughout the historic period, the study of architectural development which forms the scope of part three is directly related to the similar climatic problems of the present.

The stylistic development of the Ancient, Christian and Renaissance, and Arab-Islamic are discussed in the light of an intrinsic connection of a vernacular Mediterranean climate. The court provides the theme of both the vernacular and developed style: whether in the typical Greek or Oriental house or in the monumental religious and social expression of the *sahn* temple, or palace. Regional variation in design can be traced as structural forms developed in sympathy with the building material of the landscape. The stone trabeated classical column formation or the 'arcuated' Islamic arches on brick piers represent definite stylistic variation to the same need for adjusting semi-open spaces between the court and sheltered rooms.

The study of Islamic architecture as an expression of Mediterranean sub-tropical latitudes would help to explain to European scholarship its general unity, and the relevance of its decorative aesthetic qualities to the physical and structural requirements of climate. The effects of Islamic art on Mediterranean classical development in the Middle Ages can be traced to the influence of brick wall tradition and associated ceramic, pottery and stucco panel decoration on the vernacular stone design. A potential enrichment in the carved textured treatment of stone surfaces is reflected at its best in the Italian Quattrocento.

Relating Renaissance architecture to the effect of Southern European climate is discussed and the relevance of Albert's written work on architecture is pointed out in relation to the Mediterranean conditions of climate.

While the fourth part surveys the present problem in the light of the full impact of a northern civilisation it develops and emphasises a southern attitude and cultivates a response to natural environment. Modern means of technics and research enlightened by the art legacy of the past serve to create in architecture a new symbolic expression of space and time.

There is a wide scope in the new civilisation for a coordinated regional planning towards a healthier environment. New agricultural village settlements need not be alien in expression to the climate and physical surroundings. The scattered type of 'garden city' development is compared unfavourably with the Mediterranean pattern of a grouped formation. The court theme such as that of the Pompeian house rather than the sporadic grouping of the European cottage type is capable of imaginatively sympathetic variation in housing schemes and civic composition.

Among the cooling amenities in civic design is the significance of water display and the fountain symbol in Mediterranean architecture. Mass composition in relation to adjust a natural and effective cooling ventilation is discussed and the wind turret, the '*bageer*' as a means for such purpose is also pointed out with a view to future possibilities of development. The hest stress, resistance to moisture and light reflection are aspects to be related to building material. Developing the cultivated use of primary building materials such as stone, brick, mortar and timber in accord with technical and aesthetic climatic considerations is to be directed, and with a revived associated craftsmanship and skilled building labour a trend towards a better climatically suited structural design than the present indiscriminate use of steel framework and reinforced concrete would be realised by a conductive policy.

Reinforced concrete can be used with great advantage for foundations and it has a great part to play in connection with sub-soil movements and the pile method of construction in the plain regions where its services can be used to help maintain and develop the clay, brick and ceramic art tradition.

A final chapter summarises the various elements of composition in relation to the Mediterranean climate.

A book of illustrations is included as an appendix to show various aspects of vernacular and stylistic development in the conditions of Mediterranean climate; mainly that of Islamic architecture and its detailed elements. The bibliography also includes the principal works of Islamic architectural reference.

APPENDIX II

LECTURE TO ROYAL INSTITUTE OF BRITISH ARCHITECTS, 31 JANUARY 1984

Arab Architecture Past and Present

MY GENERATION IS UNIQUE, in one respect at least; we have lived the Mediaeval, the Modern and the Post-modern in one lifespan. I feel that I not only belong to but have lived through the past and the present, learning from both: a Baghdad in whose childhood there was a way of life with a clear identity and intent that influenced behaviour. Such clarity of intent influenced intuitional conduct of the good and the bad, and reflected the 'traditional image of the environment', an environment where people and architecture were one, where there was no stage without actors and they were not just spectators.

Bred in technology, like any other person of my generation, I was led to view science and technology as knowledge and reminded by my parents of the saying of the Prophet, 'Seek knowledge even if you have to go to China for it,' and the seventh-century saying of the great Khalifa Imam Ali: 'Science is your religion which you are committed to.'

The theme of 'Arab Architecture, Past and Present' should be seen in the light of rather 'Arab Architecture Past, and Modern Buildings in Arab Countries' where the latter is in search of Arab identity. I do not intend to draw on the polemics of tradition versus modernism. Enough has been said on the virtues of each and the same questions remain unanswered.

I shall begin with an attempted definition of my understanding of the nature of Islamic architecture, and I shall attempt to show what characterises architecture as Islamic at the end of the twentieth century.

Then I propose to follow six types of questions or issues that would relate to the practising architect in the Arab region of the Muslim world.

1. How does one unify traditional urbanism with modern urbanism?
2. How does one envisage the status of the Mosque in urban city planning?
3. With relation to new urban design and its relevance to traditional continuity how can an airport or a street have an Islamic or Arab character?
4. How can a high-rise building of contemporary practice acquire a local identity?
5. How to interpret the attitude of traditional continuity relevant to Islamic traditional form and its place in the design rationale of the aesthetic of international contemporary practice in the Arab world?

The response to the issue would be seen in the light of the dialogue and visual presentation. This might be followed by clarifying additional questions. Prior to this visual dialogue, I will point out considerations relevant to design appreciation and practice associated with the meaning of Islamic architecture.

What is Islamic architecture? Unity which transcends different regions and periods has been achieved and expressed in the built-up environment of the Muslim world. Different races and traditions were brought together by the common belief and brotherhood of the faith. Islam was not only a religion but a way of life. The ethical code was seen in man's relations to one another and his obedience to One God, the Architect and Master Builder of the Universe. This is reflected in man's behaviour in everyday life and his built-up environment wherever he would be. Orientation to the focal point of Mecca, the concept of the 'mihrab' is a fundamental symbol of the Islamic faith.

The specific geographic location of the Arab world, a region south of the Mediterranean and Europe, gives it a local latitude, where the freedom and movement of traders, who travelled from Byzantium to China, gave a cultural, ethical and social unity to the formation of Islamic architecture. For instance, although the dome of a Mosque in Egypt might differ from one in India or Morocco, no one can deny that each is fundamentally Islamic in design.

The contrast between the sacred and secular was not so significant. The Mosque and the suq lived together harmoniously, Their expression in the built-up environment is one of the most notable features in the southern Mediterranean area. The rich and the poor lived together in the urban environment where the large house and small were adjoining one another. The large house with its greater function extended horizontally, never vertically. The codes of everyday life were intuitional and customs and traditions prevailed. The large house, and those who were blessed high incomes, would have had part of their house open to the neighbourhood. From this, developed the concept of the 'diwan' or reception part of the large house which would represent a sort of audience hall for the neighbourhood.

Similarly in terms of architectural design the large and the small, the large scale and the domestic of space structure co-existed. This is almost the highest aesthetic quality found in this architecture.

Monumentality is not aggressive or consciously present. It is rather an opulence of social space needed where people are inseparable from buildings. The grandeur of the vaulted shelter encompasses a large constant by the use of a 2-metre-high arched doorway. Thus dominance is subject to human scale reference. If height is there, it should be there for a worthy purpose suited to a reality which concerns the masses and not the individual on account of the masses. The small scale also acts as a relief to emphasise the grand. If the grand persists, there has to be a compromise. If the city of skyscrapers has to be there, the question one must ask is what the human scale can do to impose its order on the situation.

The concept of space brought about an inwardness in the style of a traditional house. The outer elevation was not even considered. The inner space around the central courtyard provided the intermediate spaces of the semi-covered with the covered, and a balance of such relationships between the open, the semi-open, and the closed was the design criterion applied.

From this, the elements such as the wall, the gate and the interior itself gained specific characteristics in the whole identity of the building. Consequently secondary elements in Islamic architecture came to be independent from the whole, but the single elements of motifs of each were not to detract attention from the overall surface or create emphasis. Hence unity in diversity in architectural terms became the theme.

The language of the Qur'an, the Arabic script and the art of calligraphy were applied to all crafts and buildings, acting as unifying factors, which will always distinguish Islamic architecture anywhere and at any time. Since Islam does not encourage pictorial representation, the language of the Qur'an, the Word, became the legitimate artistic device the craftsman could utilise.

Geometric and Arabesque forms developed into Islamic art and architecture as other artistic devices available to the artist since they were abstract representations and not pictorial. These abstract forms left design freer to changes and offered tremendous variety to the applied arts.

It is the nature of such an appreciation that Islamic architecture should be seen as an environmental concern where architectural excellence is only part of the whole. The ethical, cultural and time values worked together, not as separate entities. These were the principles from which I have found my guidelines and scale of reference in my design practice.

To conclude I would like to add the following.

Unity in diversity at the global level should lead towards a new phase which would widen the local and the indigenous to possess an international status of an identified quality. Such a new identity would bear on integration that extends beyond the vernacular of the past.

Modernism as practised in Arab regions is rigid and backward in its discipline of functionalism. Traditional design forms provide more flexibility regarding multi-use, and a simplicity with richness, peace and dignity. Richness becomes human in its aptitude where personal identity is not the only focus of interest and there is no need to be in the spotlight. Thus, here is the essence of 'more could be less' – the more providing enriched human scale and art and craft involvement: the less in the oneness inherent in the sublime meaning of unity. The outcome of such rich unity would be 'simplicity with dignity'.

Traditional continuity should mean quality control in the built-up environment. 'To seek delight a Holy Trinity' should translate to include aspirations, identity, human scale and time dimensions which are a functional demand of the mind and the spirit. Creativity in urban design and details should be a highly cultivated training and aptitude instinct that identifies the human race.

We learn to look and cultivate vision, and the vocabulary is there in nature, the source of all arts, and the experiences of our past generations are starting points and stimuli be continued. This faculty of thinking now should be free from inhibition, relaxing in contemplation, tolerant to disregard art assertion, learning to see not only part of the truth but the whole truth.

Within such guidelines, the architect is left to be not only the composer of the symphony, but also the conductor and he cannot afford to be anything less. It is a role not to be envied, a role not of display and arrogance and the limited vision of cultural assertion. It is a role for the survival of the quality of life in the design environment.

It is the ideology of the human scale which gives the guiding route. Traditional continuity should not mean living in the past. It should be a question of the past living in the present for a better future.

APPENDIX III

ADDRESS TO *THE CENTENARY OF THE IRAQI ARCHITECT MOHAMED MAKIYA* HELD IN CONJUNCTION WITH THE BAGHDAD CAPITAL OF CULTURE FESTIVITIES IN 2014

DEAR FRIENDS AND LOVED ONES in Baghdad who are of the soul and conscience of this great city, it is my honour to address you. Even though I am 100 years old I would have liked to meet you and I would have found comfort in seeing your faces and hearing your words.

Baghdad, my dear friends, is a pearl of the pearls of the age. It might become ill and tired, moan of illness, but it doesn't get old, for the time of great cities is different from our modern understanding of time.

Cities have souls, and these are tangible souls that can be sniffed and sensed, in every place. Baghdad is dear and priceless. When we were forced to leave it, many years ago, we knew that some of our soul stayed there on the banks of the Tigris, in the city's alleyways, coffee-shops, balconies and squares. We knew that we had part of Baghdad with us. It grew with us like our children. We grew old and to a ripe old age. This centenary is on its way out, but that thing, that part of Baghdad, will not grow old. It is not going to get to a ripe old age. It is united with our dreams, our dialect, our way of thinking. It climbs the walls of our houses. It metamorphoses into a kind Iraqi sun that is warm in the severe cold winter days and provides a nice cold breeze from the Tigris during summer days.

Cities are our doubles. They leave their imprints on our souls. But not all cities do that, only some – and Baghdad is one of them.

Architecture, in its essence, is intimately related to place, history, function, people. The place gives us part of itself and that means that we should always think for its own sake, be creative for its own sake, and be proud of belonging to it. It is regrettable that Baghdad has been disfigured for decades. It is regrettable that the architecture did not always belong to that authentic relationship with the river, its banks and the soul that is living between them.

I entrust Baghdad to you. Listen to her. Listen to her voice repeatedly. You will discover it in the movement of the trees and date palms, in the flow of the river water, in the pure laughter. Contemplate her colour. You will find it in the bricks, in the wood, in the blue colour of the water, in the brown colour of our people.

Al-Kufa Gallery, with all of the heritage and history which it had recorded over decades, belongs to Baghdad. That is why I request that Al-Kufa Gallery should be returned to its natural place in Baghdad. And because my hundred years will not enable me to realise this task myself, I have asked my son, Kanan, to work with you on this matter.

I send you, my friends sons and grandsons, all my love, respect and gratitude. Take care of Baghdad so that Baghdad will take care of you. Take care of Iraq which gave us a lot, despite all the pain.

NOTES

CHAPTER 1

'I never had to read about a medieval city...'
Mohamed Makiya talking to Guy Mannes-Abbott

1. Makiya told Lawrence Weschler (*Calamities of Exile*, p. 5) that 'he was born on the tenth of Muharram, which is the holiest day in the Shiite calendar – the anniversary of the defeat, in AD 680, of Husayn, the son of Ali, whom Shiites consider the true heir of the Prophet, and whose massacre outside Karbala brought about the schism between Shia and Sunni Islam.'
2. Marozzi, *Baghdad: City of Peace, City of Blood*, p. 290.
3. Mannes-Abbott, 'Deeply Baghdadi', p. 63.
4. Maureen Kubba began writing a biography of Mohamed Makiya that she never completed.
5. Quoted in Mannes-Abbott, 'Deeply Baghdadi'.
6. Ibid.
7. Ibid.

CHAPTER 2

'When I started my schooling...'
Mohamed Makiya talking to Guy Mannes-Abbott

1. Crinson, *Modern Architecture and the End of Empire*, pp. 32, 33.
2. Wren is one of the most highly acclaimed architects in English history, who rebuilt fifty-two churches after the great fire of London in 1666 and also designed St Paul's Cathedral. Inigo Jones was the first significant architect of Welsh ancestry to employ Vitruvian rules of proportion and symmetry (based on designs in nature) in buildings.
3. Al-Khayoun, *Reflections on the Years*, p. 127.

CHAPTER 3

'I was lucky enough to study for a PhD...'
Mohamed Makiya talking to Al-Khayoun

1. A letter from a Mr Burges in the Home Office (Aliens Department) to a Mr Crosthwaite in the Foreign Office, dated 24 February 1943, stated:

> With reference to your letter of the 29th [of] September last regarding 17 Iraqi students in this country some of whom had refused travel back to Iraq, we have ascertained that they are all now more or less usefully employed except [for] three: viz.
>
> (1) M. Salam
> (2) Mohamed S. Makiya
> (3) Rahim Attar
>
> Makiya is studying at Cambridge and is described as a good, painstaking student. He says he is not permitted by the Iraqi Government to take employment; if he cannot be permitted to continue his studies he would like to return to his own country. It is proposed to leave him to his studies for the time being. In these two cases (Salam and Makiya), the Iraqi Government has apparently not withdrawn its financial support. In light of all the circumstances, there appears to be no need at present to contemplate the exercise of pressure in any of these cases to ensure that these men leave the United Kingdom, but the cases of Makiya and Rahim Attar will continue to be watched.

2. Weschler, *Calamities of Exile*, pp. 151–2.

CHAPTER 4

'When I left Iraq, it was in the Middle Ages...'
Mohamed Makiya talking to Guy Mannes-Abbott

1. Al-Khayoun, *Reflections on the Years*, pp. 153–4.
2. Weschler, *Calamities of Exile*, p. 8.

NOTES

CHAPTER 5

'The thing that was good for people in Iraq was the social life. . .'
Margaret Makiya talking to her granddaughter, Bushra.

1. Cohen, *What's Left?*, p. 21.
2. Hind Makiya died on 14 March 2016 of a heart attack. She had thirteen mini-strokes starting in the 1980s and throughout 2011.
3. Makiya, *Post-Islamic Classicism*, p. 32.
4. Mannes-Abbott, 'Deeply Baghdadi', p. 61.
5. Ibid.

CHAPTER 6

'I was a stranger [to Iraqi artists in the fifties] because I am not a painter. . .'
Mohamed Makiya talking to Guy Mannes-Abbott

1. De Gaury, *Three Kings in Baghdad: The Tragedy of Iraq's Monarchy*, pp. 79–81.
2. Makiya, *Post-Islamic Classicism*, p. 11.
3. Al-Khalil, *The Monument*, p. 83.
4. Mannes-Abbott, 'Deeply Baghdadi', p. 60.
5. Malek, *Makikya Collection of Modern Arab Art*, p. 1.
6. Malek, *The Dr Mohamed Makiya and Kufa Collection of Works by Jewad Salim*, p. 8.

CHAPTER 7

'I had to build a cathedral in an area suitable for a chapel.'
Mohamed Makiya, quoted in Post Islamic Classicism by Kanan Makiya

1. Makiya, *Post-Islamic Classicism*, p. 13.
2. Ibid, p. 16.

CHAPTER 8

*'The architecture school drastically changed
the training of Iraqi architects...'*
Panayiota Pyla, Landscapes of Development

1. Quoted in Mannes-Abbott, 'Deeply Baghdadi'.
2. Towe, 'Islamic Architecture Has "Principals [sic] of Faith"'.
3. Al-Khayoun, *Reflections on the Years*, pp. 178–79.
4. Cohen, *What's Left?*, p. 23.

CHAPTER 9

*'I was like Isabel Burton [wife of the legendary British explorer]. Pay, pack
and follow – that was her motto, and it became mine.'*
Margaret Makiya, quoted in Lawrence Weschler, Calamities of Exile

1. Weschler, *Calamities of Exile*, p. 17.
2. Zina Allawi remembers that her father was, like Makiya, accused of involvement in Freemasonry. This contradicts the account in Nick Cohen's book. Allawi's father went to prison for his alleged Masonic activities but was released. Makiya was in Bahrain when this happened and did not return to Iraq.

CHAPTER 10

'Traditional continuity should not mean living in the past...'
Mohamed Makiya, lecture to Royal Institute of British Architects

1. Dates refer to the completion date of the project.
2. Makiya, *Post-Islamic Classicism*, pp. 30–32.
3. Aga Khan Trust for Culture, 'Gateway to Isa Town, Isa Town, Bahrain', https://archnet.org/sites/454.
4. Hegazy, 'Continuity and Change of Muscat House', p. 98.
5. Ibid, pp. 65–66.

6. Parkyn, 'The Arab Consultants', p. 35.
7. Makiya, *Post-Islamic Classicism*, p. 75.

CHAPTER 11

'This is for history. It's not for the people there now...'
Mohamed Makiya, quoted in Lawrence Weschler, Calamities of Exile

1. Al-Khalil (aka Makiya), *The Monument*, p. 60.
2. Mannes-Abbott, 'Deeply Baghdadi', p. 61.
3. Makiya, *Post-Islamic Classicism*, p. 131.
4. Ibid, p. 106.
5. Ibid, p. 134.
6. Weschler, *Calamities of Exile*, pp. 60–61.

CHAPTER 12

'The most important thing in our lives is heritage...'
Mohamed Makiya, quoted in an introduction to the Kufa Gallery

1. Abdul Rahim Hassan, *Al-Aalam* magazine, Issue No. 193 (24 October 1978), pp. 52–54.
2. Makiya made some cassette recordings of his memories and his thoughts on architecture, which were never transcribed; he dictated them to Rashid al-Khayoun, who transcribed them and published them in *Reflections on the Years*.
3. Mannes-Abbott, 'Deeply Baghdadi', p. 63.

CHAPTER 13

'I am a conductor without an orchestra.'
Mohamed Makiya, remark to friends and colleagues

CHAPTER 14

'The Makiya name is a legacy in itself.'
Diddi Malek, Makiya's assistant, interview with author

1. Mohamed Makiya, 1914–2015, https://archnet.org/authorities/13.

POSTSCRIPT

1. According to Antiwar.com.
2. Maikya, *The Rope*, p. 303.
3. Ibid, p. 300.
4. Lecture to Royal Institute of British Architects, 31 January 1984.

BIBLIOGRAPHY

Allawi, Ali: *Faisal I of Iraq*, Yale University Press, 2014.

Al-Khalil, Samir (aka Kanan Makiya): *The Monument: Art, Vulgarity and Responsibility in Iraq*, Andre Deutsch, London, 1991.

Al-Khayoun, Rashid: *Reflections on the Years; Biography of an architecture and the Diary of a Baghdadi Neighbourhood*, Saqi Books, London, 2015.

Al-Said, Ahmed Naji: *Contemporary Iraqi Art: A Journey with the Iraqi Architect Mohammed Makiya* (unpublished manuscript).

Al-Sultani, Khalid: *Mohammad Makiya: A Century of Architecture and Life*, Adib Books, Jordan, 2014.

Cohen, Nick: *What's Left? How the Liberals Lost their Way*, Chapter One, 'An Iraqi Solzhenitsyn', HarperCollins, 2007.

Crinson, Mark: *Modern Architecture and the End of Empire*, Ashgate Publishing, UK, 2003.

Dabrowska, Karen: *Iraq: The Ancient Sites & Iraqi Kurdistan*, Bradt Travel Guides, UK, 2015.

Damluji, Salma Samar: *The Architecture of Oman*, Ithaca Press, UK, 1998.

De Gaury, Gerald: *Three Kings in Baghdad: The Tragedy of Iraq's Monarchy*, I.B. Tauris, London, 1961.

Hegazy, Soheir Mohamed: 'Continuity and Change of a Muscat House: Influencing Factors and Responses', *International Journal of Advanced Research* (2015), Volume 3, Issue 9.

Hourani, Albert: *A history of the Arab Peoples*, Faber & Faber, London 2005.

Hughes, Quentin: *Seaport: Architecture and Townscape in Liverpool*, Lund Humphries, London, 1964.

Makiya, Kanan: *Post-Islamic Classicism: A Visual Essay on the Architecture of Mohamed Makiya*, Saqi Books, London 1990.

Makiya, Kanan: *The Rope*, Pantheon Books, New York, 2016.

Malek, Diddi (ed): *Makiya Collection of Modern Arab Art*, Andy Barklem, London, 2014.

Malek, Diddi (ed): *The Dr Mohamed Makiya and Kufa Collection of Works by Jewad Salim*, Andy Barklem, London, 2013.

Mannes-Abbott, Guy: 'Deeply Baghdadi', interview with Mohamed Makiya in *Bedoun* Magazine, Summer 2009.

Marozzi, Justin: *Baghdad City of Peace, City of Blood*, Penguin Books, UK, 2015.

Parkyn, Neil: 'The Arab Consultants. Mohamed Makiya', Middle East Construction, November 1983.

Pyla, Panayiota: Landscapes of Development: The Impact of Modernization Discourses on the Physical Environment of the Eastern Mediterranean, Harvard University Press, 2013.

Reilly, C. H.: *Scaffolding in the Sky: A Semi-Architectural Autobiography*, George Routledge & Sons Ltd, London, 1938.

Stark, Freya: *Baghdad Sketches*, Tauris Parke paperbacks, London, 2011.

Thistlewood, David: *Insight*, Liverpool University Magazine, Autumn 2008.

Thomas, Gavin: *The Rough Guide to Oman*, Rough Guides.

Towe, Sara, 'Islamic architecture has "principals [sic] of faith"', *Middle East Times*, 1984.

Weschler, Lawrence: *Calamities of Exile*, University of Chicago Press, 1998.

INDEX

References to images are in *italics*; references to notes are indicated by n.

Abbasids 2, 64, 139–40
Abboud, Chafic 153
Abdul-Mahdi, Adil 173
Abd al-Ilah, Prince 9, 39
Aboo, Faraj 84
Abu Qlam (Baghdad) 40–1
Adnan, Etel 153
Aga Khan 4
Ali, Jawad 17
Ali, Mahdi 178, 179, 180, 188–9
al-Ali, Naji 152
Allameddin, Ida 153
Allawi, Ja'far 23, 24, 26
Allawi, Yasmine 105, 168, 180–1
Allawi, Zina 105, 111, 112–13, 120, 123
   and Freemasons 216n2
   and Heinle-Wischer 131–2
   and Makiya legacy 199
   and Quad Design 158–9
Alwash, Dhikra 186
al-Alwiya (Baghdad) 51
Amer, Essam 158
anti-Semitism 27
Arab architecture *see* Islam
Arab culture 46
Arab League headquarters (Tunis) 107, 120–2
Arabesque 60, 73
archaeology 53, 86–7
Archicentre 126

architecture 56–7, 67–8, 80–2, 96
   and art 60
   and awards 187–8, 196
   and Bahrain 107–10
   and climate 34, 36–7, 202–4
   and Islam 37–8, 205–9
   and Middle Eastern 2, 24, 46, 123–5
   see also Makiya Associates; mosques; School of Architecture
Arif, Abd al-Salam 99, 100
Arif, Maj Gen Abdul Rahman 100–1
art 3, 60–5, 68–73, 84, 145–6; *see also* Kufa Gallery
Artymowska, Zofia 82
Assyria 60, 64
Awni, Kahtan 65
Azzawi, Dia 153, 162
al-Azzawi, Subhi 77, 85, 128, 170, 185
   and Kufa Gallery 155, 156

Baath Socialist Party 2, 23, 93–4, 130, 171
   and coups 67, 100–1
   see also Saddam Hussein
Babylon 60, 94
Badeea, Princess 47
Badran, Rasem 141–2

al-Badri, Sami 156
Baghdad 1–2, 5, 7–9, 172–4, 185–7, 192–4
  and Arab Baath Socialist Party headquarters 130
  and architecture 56–7, 64
  and art 70–1
  and capital of culture 210–11
  and green belt 43
  and Hitawin 46–7
  and Makiya Consultancy Committee 195–6
  and Mansour 55–6
  and map *11*
  and Margaret 49–51, 52–3
  and modernisation 57–9, 66–7
  and Non-Aligned Nations Conference 129
  and return 40–1
  and State Mosque 133, 135–42, 145
  and university 23, 42, 80–1, 82, 96–9
  see also Department of Architecture (Baghdad University); Khulafa Mosque; Sabbabigh al-Aal; School of Architecture
Baghdad (Makiya) 71
al-Baghdadi, Abu Bakr 179
Bahrain 90, 94, 106, 107–10
al-Bakr, Ahmad Hassan 100, 103
Barrage, Fadi 153
Basra 9, 154
al-Bassam, Sadiq 18, 41
Bayt Greizah (Muscat) *114*, 115
al-Bazzaz, Abdul Rahman 23
Beckett, Andy 160–1
Bell, Gertrude 19, 51
Bigham, Julia 154

Bofill, Ricardo 135–6
Britain *see* Great Britain
British Council 52, 65
Budden, Lionel 26–7
builders 46–7, 78

Cairo 39, 48
Caliph's Mosque (Baghdad) 75
calligraphy 3, 60, 73, 126–7, 154, 208
Cambridge *see* King's College, Cambridge
Čejka, Jan 82
Ceremonial Parade Grounds (Tikrit) 142–5
Chadirji, Rifat 61, 64, 65, 70, 156, 188
Chamberlain, Neville 21
China 13, 29–30
Christians 9
Christie, Agatha 19, 65
cinema 22–3
climate 34, 36–7, 202–4
Cohen, Nick: *What's Left? How Liberals Lost Their Way* 50, 216n2
College of Jurisprudence (Baghdad) 96
College of Theology (Baghdad) 96
Conant, Rupert 154
concrete 125–6, 127–8, 204
Cotswolds 84, 157, *158*, 160–1
Crawford, Margaret *see* Makiya, Margaret
Crinson, Mark: *Modern Architecture and the End of Empire* 24–5
Critchley, Doris 51

Damluji, Salma Samar: *The*

Architecture of Oman 115–16
al-Daoud, Ibrahim 101
Daraie, Mohammad-Reza 111, 158
Dawa Party 134, 175
Dawood, Yousuf 110
Department of Architecture (Baghdad University) 3, 4
Development Board 57–8, 65
Directorate General of Municipalities 42–3, 45
Directorate of the Baghdad Water Board 96
Doha (Qatar) 108
Douaihy, Saliba 153
Doxiadis, Constantinos Apostolou 57, 65, 68
Dubai 108, 185
Dujailli, Hassan 23

Eden, William Arthur 26
Egypt 19, 39, 48, 207
El Hajj, Fatima 153
El Rawas, Mohammed 153

Faisal I of Iraq, King 9, 57, 58
Faisal II of Iraq, King 9, 63
al-Farabi 152
Faraj, *Ustad* Hasan 47
Fatimids 39, 65
Fethi, Ihsan: *Traditional Houses in Baghdad* 7
First World War 7, 8
France 19–20
Freedom Monument (Nasb al-Hurriyah) (Baghdad) 70
Freemasons 103, 137, 216n2

al-Gailani, Lamia 156, 198
Gaspard, André 149
Gaury, Gerald de: *Three Kings in Baghdad: The Tragedy of Iraq's Monarchy* 66–7
Germany 27, 28
Ghani Hikmat, Muhammad 65, 71, 73, 84, 162
Ghazi I of Iraq, King 9
Ghoussoub, Mai 149–50, 151, 152, 153, 165
Gilgamesh 164
Golan Heights 154
Great Britain 2, 7, 8–9, 18, 21–2, 97
 and art 61
 and Cotswolds 84, 157, *158*, 160–1
 and Makiya 81–2
 and maps 43
 and Oman 114
 and Portsmouth Treaty 41
 and Saddam Hussein 170
 see also King's College, Cambridge; Liverpool School of Architecture; London
Gropius, Walter *56*, 57, 68
Guiragossian, Paul 153
Gulf, the 2; *see also* Bahrain; Kuwait; Oman; Qatar; Saudi Arabia; United Arab Emirates
Guthrie, Shirley 156

Habibi, Emile 156
Haddad, Muhammad 126–7
Hadi, Sayed 46
Hadid, Muhammad 89
Hadid, Zaha 89, 181
al-Haidari, Ibrahim 176, 188
Haider, Kadhim 65
Haider, Saleh Mahdi 23
al-Haideri, Bulland 62
Hakim, Besim 155
al-Hakim, Mahdi 148–9

Hamoudi, *Ustad* 47
Hassan, Abdul Rahim 95, 176, 188, 190
Hassan, Faiq 20, 71, 70
   and Iraqi Artists' Society 61, 62, 65
Hassan, Kasim 89
Hassan, Zaki Muhammad 65
Hatra 53, 86–7
Haylock, John 62
Hazelton, Fran 164
Heaps, Godfrey 111, 120–2, 142–3, 158
Hegazy, Soheir Mohamed 115
Heinle, Wischer und Partner 122, 131–2
Henry VI of England, King 33
Hosseini, Reza 154
al-Huda, Bint 135
Humanitarian Dialogue Foundation (Salam House) *183*, 184, 192
al-Hursi, Sati 18
Hussein, Imam 12, 74

India 156–7, 207
Iran 41, 132, 133, 135–6, 137, 166–7
Iraq 2, 9, 25, 147, 195
   and architecture 84–5
   and art 154, 156
   and education funding 32–3
   and Erbil *121*, 122–3, 131, 132–3
   and Iran war 135–6
   and Kufa 150–1
   and Makiya 177–9, 191–2
   and maps 42–3
   and monarchy 67
   and politics 41–2, 99–101
   and Second World War 27, 30
   and Tikrit 142–5
   see also Baghdad; Saddam Hussein
Iraq Memory Foundation (IMF) 104, 171–2, 173
Iraqi Academic Association 94
Iraqi Artists' Society 3, 60–5, 68–70, 71
Isa Town Gateway (Bahrain) 107, 109–10
ISIS 179, 191
Islam 37–8
   and architecture 46, 79, 83, 205–9
   see also Qur'an; Shi'i Islam; Sunni Islam
Israel 34, 36, 152
al-Issa, Abdul Razzaq Abdul Jaleel 94–5
Issa, Rose 151, 152, 153, 161–2, 165

al-Jaafari, Ibrahim 173
Jacobs, David 156
al-Jadir, Khalid 61
Jami'yat al-Ruwad (Pioneers Group) 62, 65
Jawad, Mustafa 17, 71
Jews 9, 12, 27, 34, 102
Jones, Inigo 25, 38, 213n2
Joseph, Lilly 52, 101
al-Jumaie, Saleh 153

Kadhimiya 85
al-Kahoun, Rashid 88
Kamel, Abdallah Ihsan 89
Karbala 43, 85, 96, 156
Kashi, Dia 50, 157, 178, 179, 190, 198
al-Kashtini, Khalid 164, 175–6
Kasraian, Nasrollah 154
Katah Bridge (Baghdad) *16*

Index

al-Kazimy, Mustafa 90, 172–4, 175, 178, 189, 192
Kazzar, Nazim 103
Khairallah Talfah, Gen Adnan 103, 104
al-Khalili, Sadiq 50
al-Khayoun, Rashid 26, 27, 37, 155
Reflections on the Years: Biography of an Architect and the Diary of a Baghdadi Neighbourhood 10, 12, 185, 217n2
Khazaraji, Walid 165, 166
Khulafa Mosque (Baghdad) 2, 4, 47, 74–9, 184, 186
King's College, Cambridge 31, 32–9
Kite, Stephen 122–3, 132
Kubba, Maureen 13, 23
Kufa Gallery (London) 2, 3, 4, 150–7, 161–5, 166
  and Baghdad 195–6
  and closure 174–6, 177
  and Iraqi opposition 149
  and Makiya legacy 198
Kufa Makiya Trust and Charity 196–7
Kufa University 93–5
Kurdistan 30, 53–5, 154
Kurds 100, 144, 169
Kuwait 108, 129, 166–7, 168
  and State Mosque 87, 107, 111, 125–8

Lane, Alan 62
Laski, Harold 34
Lawrence, A. W. 37
Le Corbusier 57, 68
Lebanon 149, 152, 153
lectures 155–6
Lister, Richard 52

Liverpool School of Architecture 23–31, *44*
London 22–3, 39
  and Makiya Associates 111–13, 116–17, 118–20, 123–5
  see also Kufa Gallery
Lorna Selim (family home) 15, *16*, 17
Lynch, Lt Henry 8
Lynch Company 13

McLuhan, Marshall 152
Ma'dan (marsh Arabs) 53, 54
al-Madfai, Qahtan 61, 64, 82, 186
Madloum, Midhat Ali 17, 26, 64, 82
Majlis al-Ia'mar 178–9
Makhzoumi, Jala 84
Makiya, Abdul Aziz (brother) 12, 17, 18, 35
Makiya, Aboud (uncle) 14
Makiya, Amal (niece) 10, 36, 49, 51, 162
Makiya, Bahiya (mother) 12
Makiya, Bushra (granddaughter) 52, 72, 96, 97, 98, 181
Makiya, Ghassan (nephew) 148
Makiya, Hind (daughter) 36, 51–3, 55, 56, 101–2, 149
Makiya, Kanan (son) 36, 51–4, 55–6, 101, 110–11
  and Baghdad 173–4
  and Baghdad State Mosque 137, 141
  and 'Charter 91' 167–8
  and father 189–90, 191–2
  and IMF 171–2
  and Khulafa Mosque 74, 75–6, 78–9
  and Kufa Gallery 152, 166,

175–6
and Kuwait State Mosque 125, 126, 127–8
and library 197
and Makiya Associates 129, 130, 131
and MIT 182–4
The Monument: Art, Vulgarity and Responsibility in Iraq 70, 135
and mother 117–18
Post-Islamic Classicism 60, 67
Republic of Fear 129, 133, 138–9, 146–7
The Rope 181, 194–5
and Saqi Books 149–50, 151
and School of Architecture 90
and Tikrit Parade Grounds 144
Makiya, Mahdi (uncle) 13
Makiya, Margaret (wife) 31, 32, 35–6, 49–53, 54
and death 181, 189
and depression 117–18, 119, 174–5
and exile 94
and ill health 179–80
and library 196–7
and Oman 116
and politics 103–4, 105–6
and teaching 96–8, 99
Makiya, Mohamed 1–5, 7, 80–2, 160–1, 202–4
and Arab architecture 205–9
and architects 57, 110–13
and art 61–4, 68–73, 145–6
and Baghdad 40–1, 58–65, 67, 172–4
and Baghdad State Mosque 136–42
and Cambridge 32–3, 34–9

and centenary address 210–11
and death 188–90
and Directorate General of Muncipalities 42–3, 45
and education 17–18
and Europe 19–20
and family 181–2
and the Gulf 107–10
and ill health 174–5, 176, 177, 180–1
and Iraq 167, 168–9, 170, 178–9, 191–2
and Kanan 146–7
and Khulafa Mosque 74–9
and Kufa 93–5
and Kufa Gallery 150–7, 161–4, 166
and Kuwait State Mosque 125–8
and legacy 195–6, 197–9
and library 104–5, 196–7
and Liverpool 23–7, 29–31
and London 21–3, 118–19
and Makiya Associates 45–8
and marriage 49–50, 179–80
and Martin 129–31
and MIT 182–4
and Muscat 114–16
and politics 103–4
and Rashid University 122–3
and recognition 185–8
and Saddam Hussein 148–9
and Salam House 184–5
and School of Architecture 82–90, *91*, 92–3
and Sultan Qaboos Grand Mosque 158–60
and Tikrit Parade Grounds 142–3
and travelling *100*, 101–2

Index

and Tunis 120–2
and upbringing 9–10, 12–15
Makiya, Naseem (grandson) 54, 181–2
Makiya, Nazar (nephew) 110, 148
Makiya, Saleh Aziz (father) 9–10, 12–14
Makiya, Wallada (daughter-in-law) 53
Makiya Associates *44*, 45–8, 90, 110–13, 129–31
 and closure 148
 and the Gulf 107–10
 and London 116–17, 118–20, 123–5
al-Malaikah, Sadiq 17
Malek, Diddi 36, 72–3, 145–6, 181, 197
Mallowan, Sir Max 65
al-Mamoura ('global village' philosophy) 151–2
al-Ma'mun 75
Mannes-Abbott, Guy 9, 57, 71, 136–7
Mansour (Baghdad) 55–6
al-Mansour 140
al-Mansour Club (Baghdad) 62–3
al-Mansur, Abu Jafar 5maps 42–3
Marouf, Naji 71
Martin, Garry 111, 129–31, 132–3, 146, 180, 198
 and Baghdad State Mosque 141, 142
 and Tikrit Parade Grounds 144
Mason, Harold 25
Massachusetts Institute of Technology (MIT) 96, 102, 110, 182–4
Mediterranean architecture 34, 36–7, 39, 202–4
Mesopotamia 41, 58, 60, 135, 142, 151, 164
Michelangelo 73
Ministry of Awqaf 75, 76, 78
Ministry of Foreign Affairs (Baghdad) 96
Ministry of Municipalities (Baghdad) 96
modernism 27, 57, 58–9, 83, 209
Mongols 8
Moore, Henry 73
Morocco 207
mosques 3–4, 9, 39, 207; *see also* Baghdad: State Mosque; Khulafa Mosque; Kuwait; Sultan Qaboos Grand Mosque
Mosul 9, 47, 96, 179
Mottahedeh, Roy 156
Mousawi, Ali 83, 86, 160, 193–4
al-Mudafar, Mahmoud 93
Muscat 107, 108, 113, 114–16, 158–60
music 156–7

Nairn, Gerald and Norman 18–19
Najaf 43, 85, 156, 189
Naji al-Said, Ahmed 62, 69, 83–4, 162, 198
 and exhibitions *183*, 184–5
 Under the Palm Trees: Modern Iraqi Art with Mohamed Makiya and Jewad Selim 4
Nasiri, Rafa 153
al-Nayef, Col Abd al-Razzaq 101
Newton, Eric 34, 35
Nimrud 53

Oates, David 53, 108, 170
Ogaily, Akram 1, 87–8, 89, 186, 192

oil 8, 18, 58, 134, 167, 169–70
Olympic Club (Baghdad) 63–4
Oman 156; *see also* Muscat
Ottoman Empire 2, 8

Pakistan 41
Palestine 152, 154, 156
pan-Arabism 9
Parkyn, Neil 124–5
Persians 8
Pioneers Group *see* Jami'yat al-Ruwad
Poland 82–3
Ponti, Gio 57, 68
Pope, Martin 154

Qaboos bin Said, Sultan 114, 158
Qadir, Yousef Abdul 61, 62
Qasim, Abd al-Karim 3, 67, 69–70, 99–100
al-Qassab, Khalid 61, 62
Qatar 108, 148
Quad Design 158–9
Qur'an 23, 37, 127, 160, 188, 208

racism 32
al-Radi, Nuha 162
Rafidain Bank (Karbala) 96
Rafidain Bank (Kufa) 96
Ramzi, Nadhim 162
al-Rashid Street (Baghdad) 8, 41, 42, 47, 192
Rashid University (Erbil) *121*, 122–3, 131, 132
al-Rawi, Nouri 61
Reilly, Sir Charles 24
Richardson, Albert Edward: *The Art of Architecture* 35
al-Rikaby, Ali Haider 62–3
Roberts, David 71–2

Rothschild, Jon 149
Royal Institute of British Architects (RIBA) 2, 36, 123–4, 205–9
Ruiter, Michiel de 154
Ruskin, John 38
Russell, Bertrand 34, 35

Sabbabigh al-Aal 9–10, 15, 17, 74–5
Sabri, Atta 61
Sabri, Mahmoud 61, 62, 63
Saddam Hussein 3–4, 67, 129, 148–9, 161
  and Baghdad State Mosque 135, 136, 137, 138, 141
  and drainage programme 54–5
  and Iran 132, 133
  and Kuwait 166–7, 168–9
  and ousting 172
  and power 102–3, 104, 135, 169–70
  and Tikrit Parade Grounds 144
al-Sadr, Ayatollah Baqir 135
Sadr City (Baghdad) 68
al-Said, Nuri 41–2, 57
al-Said, Shakir Hassan 71, 141, *183*, 184
Vagabond Family 177
al-Sajjad, Ali 188
Salahaddin University (Erbil) 132–3
Salim, Jewad 20, 71, 72–3, 177–8
  and Freedom Monument 70
  and Iraqi Artists' Society 60–1, 62, *63*
  and Kufa Gallery 162–3
  Pastorale 64, 65
Salim, Lorna 61, 84
  Homage to Jewad Salim 162–3
Al Saqi Books (London) 149–50,

Index

175, 178
Sarraf, Attared 86–7, 180, 181
Saudi Arabia 107, 146
al-Sayyab, Badr Shakir 190
School of Architecture 82–90, *91*, 92–3, 192
sculpture 84
Second World War 21–2, 27–9, 30, 33–4
Selim, Naziha 61
Sert, Josep Luís 57
al-Shaikhli, Ismail 61
al-Shaikhly, Salah 175
Shaw, Edward 33
Shi'i Islam 3, 9, 13, 161, 179
   and *Ashura* 12
   and Kufa 93
   and Kufa Gallery 165
   and Russell 35
   and Saddam Hussein 135
al-Shouk, Ali 156
Shubar, Kadhim 93
al-Sikafi, Hussein 163, 176
Silk Road 9, 10, 13
al-Silq, Ghada 90, 92
al-Sistani, Grand Ayatollah Ali 179
Solagh, Bayan Jabr 173
Somalia 154
Sotheby's 105, 145, 194, 196–7
Sousa, Ahmed 71, 89
Soviet Union 101, 103
Stamp, Dudley 35
Stark, Freya 19, 51
   Baghdad Sketches 15
Stewart, Desmond 62
Stokes, Adrian: *The Quattro Cento: A Different Conception of the Italian Renaissance* 125–6
Sudan 154
Suez crisis 50

Suleiman Pasha 75
Sultan Qaboos Grand Mosque (Muscat) 107, 108, 158–60
al-Sultani, Khalid 92, 188
   Mohammad Makiya: A Century of Architecture and Life 142, 186
Sumer 60, 64
Sunni Islam 9, 179
Suq al-Ghazl Mosque (Baghdad) 75
Syria 13, 18–19, 101–2, 179

Talabani, Jalal 173, 175, 192
Tamayouz Lifetime Achievement Award 187–8
Tawfik, Umran 32, 69
textile trade 9–10, 12, 13
Thistlewood, David 24
Tigris River 15, *16*, 84, 85, 167
Trevelyan, George: *English Social History: A Survey of Six Centuries* 34
Tunisia 107, 120–2
Turkey 41; *see also* Ottoman Empire

al-Umari, Arshad 42
United Arab Emirates (UAE) 107, 108, 148
United Nations (UN) 167, 169
United States of America (USA) 167, 169, 170; *see also* Massachusetts Institute of Technology (MIT)
al'Urayidh, Jawad 110

ventilation 85
Venturi, Robert 136
Visvadeva, Jay 156

Wahbi, Maysoon 88, 177
Warren, John: *Traditional Houses in Baghdad* 7
al-Wasiti Gallery (Baghdad) 70–1
Wells, Tom 115
Weschler, Lawrence 46, 146–7
Wilson, James 25
Winter, Jihan 106
women 97–8, 153

Wood, Michael 155–6
Wren, Christopher 25, 38, 213n2
Wright, Frank Lloyd 57, 64, 67

Yemen 154

Ziadeh, Nicola 156
Zubaidi, Saad 143